WE'VE MADE IT *ea*

GW00402052

perk up

your

pension

The Pensions Advisory Service

Published in 2009 by Age Concern Books
1268 London Road, London SW16 4ER, United Kingdom
ISBN: 978 0 86242 436 7

A catalogue record for this book is available from the
British Library.

The four national Age Concerns in the UK have joined
together with Help the Aged to form new national
charities dedicated to improving the lives of older
people.

Edited by: Vanessa Plaister

Cover design by: Vincent McEvoy

Designed and typeset by: Design and Media Solutions,
Maidstone

Printed and bound in Great Britain by: Latimer Trend,
Plymouth, Devon

Mixed Sources
Product group from well-managed
forests and other controlled sources
www.fsc.org Cert no. SGS-COC-005493
© 1996 Forest Stewardship Council

Contents

Introduction

If you were to ask someone to describe pensions, it would not be surprising if they were to answer: 'Complicated!'

But pensions do not have to be complicated. What has happened is that, over many years, rules, regulations and a raft of jargon have shrouded pensions in a cloud of mystery – and, because of this air of mystery, far too many people have been turned off from thinking about pensions.

For 'pension bores' like me, this is worrying. While for many people, pensions may not be the most riveting subject, all of us need to think about what we are going to live on when works stops and retirement starts.

Retirement should be a happy time: a time to enjoy oneself. You will have extra free time – and you might want to take advantage of this to pursue hobbies, to visit family or to go on long holidays. But to do all of that, unless you have been lucky enough to win the lottery or to come into a sizeable inheritance, you will need to have saved enough while you were working to give yourself enough income during your retirement. That is what pensions are for.

And a pension is not just about income for when you get to retirement age: many plans also include a range of other benefits, such as early payment if you become too ill to work, benefits for your dependants in the event of your death before reaching pension age and tax-free cash sums in exchange for some of your pension. Pensions can provide all of this – and tax relief on your contributions too!

Try thinking of a pension as a savings plan, but a type of savings plan that is solely designed to help you to save for your retirement. It is also a savings plan in which you get tax relief on your contributions to encourage you to save. You may not be keen to lock away your savings for a long time – but that is why there are rules in place limiting when benefits can be paid and in what form.

The types of pension across which you can come broadly fall into three groups:

- pensions paid by the government;
- those set up by employers; and
- those that are sold to individuals.

This book will help you to understand how all three types work, including how you qualify for benefits, when they can be paid and how you actually get paid.

The book also explains some of the choices that you will face, what you should be thinking about and where to go if you need more help or information.

And even though it is a book about pensions, there is even a small section on the other products that you might think about using to give yourself an income when you retire.

Acknowledgement

We wish to extend our gratitude to Paul Lewis for his kind permission to use extracts form his book *Beat the Banks*, published by Age Concern, for inclusion in Chapter 6, 'Getting financial advice'. Also, we offer Paul full recognition of his suggestion for the title of this book, *Perk Up Your Pension*.

Paul's supporting work for our charity, together with his interest and provision of financial advice to older people, has been welcomed and appreciated.

The State Pension

The State Pension is made up of two parts:

- the **basic State Pension**; and
- the **State Second Pension (S2P)**.

Some people may also have entitlement to a forerunner of S2P, which was called the **Graduated Retirement Benefit (GRB) scheme**. This started in 1961, but was stopped in 1975. Any entitlement to GRB is likely to be relatively modest.

The basic State Pension is paid to people who satisfy certain **National Insurance (NI)** contribution conditions. S2P is based on your earnings. The amount of State Pension that you receive is not dependent on income and savings, but it is taxable.

The State Pension is payable from the date on which you reach **State Pension age**, whether or not you are still working. You can, however, choose to defer drawing it and receive either extra State Pension income at a later date or a lump sum, subject to certain conditions.

The first State Pension was introduced by David Lloyd George (then Chancellor of the Exchequer) in 1908. The amount provided was minimal (between 10p and

25p a week) and means-tested. The State Pension age was 70 years old – at a time when average life expectancy was only 50 years.

State Pension age

For those people born before 5 April 1950, the State Pension age is currently 65 for men and 60 for women. From 6 April 2010, the State Pension age for women will gradually increase so that, by 6 April 2020, it will be 65 for both men and women.

It is also worth noting that, between 2024 and 2046, the State Pension age for both men and women will rise to 68. Anyone born after 6 April 1959 will be affected by this change.

To check the State Pension age that applies to you, visit the Pension Service website at www.direct.gov.uk

The basic State Pension

The amount of basic State Pension to which you are entitled is based on the number of NI qualifying years that you have accumulated. A **qualifying year** is a tax year during which your earnings are more than a lower earnings limit that is set by the government.

If you do not have sufficient earnings during a year, but you are receiving certain Social Security benefits, that year may still be treated as a qualifying year. For example, this might be the case if you are:

- incapable of work because of illness or disability;
- receiving Carer's Allowance;
- getting Working Tax Credit;
- receiving Statutory Maternity Pay.

This is not an exhaustive list and there are other circumstances in which it is possible to get credits on your NI record. Check with the Pension Service if you would like further information (see Chapter 10).

If you will reach State Pension age before 6 April 2010, you will normally need a qualifying history (that is, a number of qualifying years) that is equal to 90 per cent of your working life to be entitled to the full basic State Pension. A **working life** is considered to be 49 years for a man and 44 years for a woman. This means that men normally require a qualifying history of 44 years and women require one of 39 years.

If you only partly meet the qualifying conditions, your basic State Pension will be paid pro rata. The following example demonstrates how this will be calculated.

> **Ricardo** needs a qualifying history of 44 years to get the full rate of basic State Pension – but he has only 28 qualifying years. Ricardo's entitlement will therefore be calculated as:
>
> $$\frac{28 \text{ years}}{44 \text{ years}} \times \text{the full rate of basic State Pension}$$

If you are to receive any basic State Pension, you must also have a qualifying history that covers at least a quarter of your working life. If you do not, no State Pension is payable.

If you will reach State Pension age on or after 6 April 2010, the qualifying conditions will be different. Both men and women need only to have 30 qualifying years to be entitled to a full basic State Pension and there is no minimum number of qualifying years. This means that you start building up entitlement immediately.

Home Responsibilities Protection (HRP)

Home Responsibilities Protection (HRP) was introduced in 1978 to protect the contribution records of people with certain caring responsibilities.

If you are caring for a child under the age of 16 and receiving Child Benefit, or caring for a sick or disabled person and receiving Income Support, you get HRP automatically.

If you care for someone receiving Attendance Allowance, Constant Attendance Allowance or Disability Living Allowance, or if you are a foster carer, you need to apply for HRP.

If you need to apply for HRP, contact your local Jobcentre Plus office and ask for leaflet 'How to protect your State Pension if you are looking after someone at home' and claim form CF411. To find your local Jobcentre Plus office, visit www.jobcentreplus.gov.uk *or call 0845 055 6688.*

HRP works by reducing the number of qualifying years that you need to qualify for the basic State Pension. Each year of home responsibility will be taken away from the number of qualifying years that you need – to a minimum total of 20 qualifying years.

Many women have not had the correct HRP allocated to them, so make sure, when you claim your State Pension, that the Pension Service knows the number of years during which you were getting Child Benefit. Ask the Pension Service to check that you are receiving the correct pension.

It is worth noting that you cannot get HRP for tax years during which you were working and paying women's reduced-rate NI contributions. But if you stopped work after April 1978 for at least two whole consecutive years, you will have lost the right to pay at the women's reduced rate. It is therefore possible that you became entitled to HRP for the years that followed your loss of the reduced rate. You should check your record with HM Revenue & Customs (see Chapter 10).

If you will reach State Pension age on or after 6 April 2010, HRP will have been replaced by a system of NI credits. You will be eligible for an NI credit if you are getting Child Benefit for a child who is under the age of 12, or if you are caring for 20 hours a week for a person who is getting Attendance Allowance, Constant Attendance

Allowance, or the middle or highest rate of the care component of Disability Living Allowance.

Any years for which you previously qualified for HRP will be converted into NI credit years.

> **Judith** will reach State Pension age on 6 May 2014, when she will be 62. She gave up work in her mid-20s to look after her children and returned to work after her youngest child left school. By the time that she reaches State Pension age, she should have 25 qualifying years. But during the years that she did not work, she was automatically covered by HRP, because she was receiving Child Benefit. These years will now be replaced by a system of NI credits and will credit her with a further 15 qualifying years. Judith will therefore qualify for a full basic State Pension.

Types of basic State Pension

There are four types of basic State Pension, as follows.

- **Category A** is based on your own qualifying years.

- **Category B** is based on your husband's, wife's or civil partner's NI contribution record. The maximum payable is approximately 60 per cent of the standard Category A rate. If, however, the contributor does not qualify for the full basic State Pension, the amount of Category B pension will also be reduced. At the moment, the rules mean that married men and civil partners do not qualify for a Category B pension in the same way as married women. But from 6 April 2010, this will change, and married men and civil partners will also be able to claim a Category B pension – as long as their wives or civil partners were born on or after 6 April 1950.

- **Category D** is awarded to people who reach 80 years of age and satisfy certain residency conditions, and who fail to qualify for a Category A or B pension, or receive less than the Category D rate. The 2009–10 rate for a Category D pension is £57.05 a week.

- There is also a **Category C** pension, but the only people likely to receive this are widows of men who were over the age of 65 on 5 July 1948.

If your own Category A pension – that is, the basic State Pension based on your own qualifying conditions – is less than 60 per cent of your spouse or civil partner's Category A pension, you should contact the Pension Service and claim a Category B pension, provided that your spouse or civil partner has reached his or her State Pension age. Doing so could increase the amount available to you.

If you are entitled to a Category B pension, the combined amount of your Category A and B pensions cannot exceed 60 per cent of your spouse's or civil partner's Category A pension.

David qualifies for a Category A basic State Pension of £90 a week. His wife, Lisa, qualifies for a Category A basic State Pension of £45. By claiming a Category B pension, Lisa can improve her weekly basic State Pension to £54 a week.

If you are divorced or have had your marriage (or civil partnership) annulled, you may be able to use the NI record of your former partner – up to the tax year during which your marriage or civil partnership ended – when working out your entitlement to a Category A pension, as long as you have not remarried before you reach State Pension age.

Gaps in your National Insurance (NI) record

If you have any gaps in your NI record, it may be worthwhile, if you can afford it, to pay a voluntary contribution in order to improve your basic State Pension. You must normally pay any **voluntary contributions** for missed years within six tax years of the end of the year to which they relate.

The price of a voluntary contribution will depend on the year for which you are paying and the actual year of payment. If you pay voluntary NI contributions in the same tax year for which you have a gap or during the two years immediately afterwards, the rate will be the voluntary rate declared for that year. For 2009–10, the rate is £12.05 a week.

The rate can increase after the end of the second tax year following the tax year in which the voluntary contributions were due.

In certain circumstances, however, there are special rules that allow for voluntary contributions to be paid outside this six-year window.

- If you reached State Pension age between 6 April 1998 and 24 October 2004, and you have gaps in the tax years between 1996–97 and 2001–02, you can pay for these up to 5 April 2010.

- If you have reached or will reach State Pension age between 6 April 2008 and 5 April 2015, you can pay for missing years going back to 6 April 1975, but you must already have at least 20 qualifying years. Years during which you were covered by HRP will count as a qualifying year for this purpose.

Samina reached State Pension age on 8 July 2009. Her NI record means that she is entitled to a basic State Pension of £62 a week. She is eligible to pay for three missing years in her NI record. By doing so, she will boost her State Pension by approximately £7 a week.

A word of warning: if you do have a gap in your qualifying record, paying voluntary contributions may not always be worthwhile. For example, it may be that, despite the gap in your record, you are already on course to qualify for a full basic State Pension, or it may be that paying a voluntary contribution will not improve your basic State Pension to more than you can receive by using your spouse's contribution history (see Types of basic State Pension above, on page 6).

Maureen has reached State Pension age and is entitled to a basic State Pension of £43 a week. Her husband, Frank, has also reached State Pension age and is entitled to a basic State Pension of £90 a week. Most of Maureen's qualifying shortfall is made up of years for which she cannot now pay a voluntary contribution. She does, however, have a three-year gap for which she can do so.

Paying voluntary contributions for these years would improve her basic State Pension to £50. But if Maureen were to claim a Category B pension, she would be able to improve her basic State Pension to £54 without having to pay any voluntary contribution.

If you decide that you want to pay voluntary NI contributions, HM Revenue & Customs (HMRC) will be able to give you a quote, telling you how much it will cost and explaining how payment can be made. You can contact HMRC's National Insurance Contribution Office on 0845 302 1479.

For help in deciding whether paying voluntary NI contributions is worthwhile, phone the Pensions Advisory Service on 0845 601 2923 and its advisers will explain the issues that you need to consider.

Additional State Pension

If you are in employment, you may also be building up entitlement to **additional State Pension**. Additional State Pension is based on your earnings in tax years from April 1978 up to the last complete tax year before you reach State Pension age. It is paid in addition to basic State Pension.

Between April 1978 and April 2002, the additional State Pension was known as the **State Earnings-Related Pension (SERPS)**. Since April 2002, it has been called the **State Second Pension (S2P)**. The calculation of S2P is more generous for low and moderate earners. This means that employees earning up to £31,800 (2009–10) are better off under S2P when compared to SERPS. Since April 2002, it has also become possible for people who are carers, or who have a long-term illness or disability, to qualify for S2P.

All employees earning over the lower earnings limit (£4,940 in 2009–10) for the relevant tax year will qualify for the additional State Pension unless they make alternative arrangements by joining an occupational or **personal pension** scheme that is contracted out (see Chapter 4).

You can also now build up an entitlement to additional State Pension if you have caring responsibilities, eg:

• if you are receiving Child Benefit and looking after a child under the age of 6;

• if you are entitled to Carer's Allowance and are under State Pension age;

- if you look after a sick or disabled person and qualify for HRP.

Because self-employed people pay a lower rate of NI contribution, they do not qualify for additional State Pension.

How to find out how much State Pension you will get

The simplest way in which you can get a State Pension forecast is by calling the Future Pension Centre (see Chapter 10). Its advisers will take your details over the telephone and post you a forecast.

Alternatively, you can obtain form BR19 from your local post office or from the Pension Service, complete it and return it to the Pension Service. You can also request a State Pension forecast online at www.direct.gov.uk

How to claim your State Pension

Normally, about four months before you reach State Pension age, the Pension Service will send you a retirement pack. Included in this pack will be a pension statement, telling you what you will receive, and a BR1 claim form.

To claim your State Pension, you need to complete the BR1 form and return it to the Pension Service. Alternatively, you can ring the claim line on 0800 731 7898.

If you do not receive an invitation to claim State Pension (if, for example, the Pension Service does not have your current address), you should contact its claim line on 0800 731 7898.

When claiming your State Pension, the maximum period for which it can be backdated is 12 months.

If you are aged 80 or over and you are eligible for a higher rate pension, you will not need to make a claim. The higher rate should be paid automatically.

Tax

The State Pension counts towards the calculation of your overall taxable income, but is normally paid without tax being deducted. Instead, any tax due is accounted for by adjusting the tax coding that applies to your other income – for example, from earnings or from your private pensions – which can make it seem as though you are being taxed heavily on your other sources of income.

Retiring abroad

The State Pension can be paid anywhere in the world, but you will only get annual increases on your pension if you live in a country within the European Economic Area (EEA), or a country with which the UK has a Social Security agreement that allows for increases.

Details of the countries with which the UK has a Social Security agreement or which are within the EEA can be found online at www.direct.gov.uk

Deferring the State Pension

When you reach State Pension age, you do not have to claim your State Pension; instead, you can choose to **defer payment**. It used to be the case that you could only defer claiming your pension for up to five years. Now, however, there is no limit to the length of time for which you are allowed to defer it.

If you decide not to claim your State Pension immediately, you can receive a pension at a higher rate at the time that you eventually do decide to claim. The current rate of increase is 1 per cent for each five weeks for which you put off payment. This equates to 10.4 per cent a year – that is:

$$\frac{52 \text{ weeks}}{5 \text{ weeks}} \times 1\% = 10.4\%$$

To qualify for an increase, you have to delay claiming for at least five weeks.

If you have delayed claiming State Pension for at least 12 consecutive months, you will also have the option of receiving a lump sum instead. The rate of increase that is used to calculate the cash sum is 2 per cent above the Bank of England's base rate (a rate that is reviewed monthly).

Please note that this extra State Pension is taxable in the same way as your normal State Pension. The lump sum payment is also taxable, but will be taxed at the rate that applies to your other income. This ensures that the lump sum payment will not put you into a higher tax bracket.

Joe is entitled to a State Pension of £90 a week, but delays claiming it until his 66th birthday. His State Pension is increased by 10.4 per cent and is therefore £99.36 a week when it comes into payment.

Because Joe delayed drawing his pension for 12 months, he has the option of receiving a lump sum instead of the additional income. Interest is added to this lump sum weekly. Assuming that the Bank of England base rate were 4 per cent, this would mean that Joe's pension would be increased by 0.1154 per cent a week.

After Week 1, the calculation is therefore:

£90 x 0.1154% = £90.10

After Week 2, the sum is:

(£90.10 + £90) x 0.1154% = £180.30

And so on...

Pension Credit

Pension Credit is a means-tested, tax-free payment for people aged 60 or over, regardless of their NI contribution record. It is designed to give those aged 60 and over a minimum level of income, and to give extra cash to those aged over 65 who have modest incomes and who have made savings for their retirement.

Payment of Pension Credit is not automatic and needs to be claimed.

When calculating your entitlement to Pension Credit, the first £6,000 of savings is ignored. For every £500 over £6,000, it is assumed that you earn £1 of weekly income.

From November 2009, the amount of savings ignored when working out Pension Credit rose from £6,000 to £10,000.

There are two parts to Pension Credit:

- the Guarantee Credit; and
- the Savings Credit.

The **Guarantee Credit** is payable from the age of 60. It works by topping up your weekly income to a guaranteed minimum level. For a single person, the Guarantee Credit could top up weekly income to £130.00 (2009–10). For couples, joint weekly income can be increased to £198.45 (2009–10).

The **Savings Credit** element is a little more complicated, but it is essentially a reward for those who have attempted to make additional provision for their retirement over and above the basic State Pension and who have a modest amount of income or savings. Savings Credit is payable from the age of 65.

People are likely to be entitled to get some money from the Savings Credit element if they have income, including their State Pension, of up to about £181 a week (if they are single) or up to £266 a week (for couples). Savings Credit is currently worth up to £20.40 a week for a single person and £27.03 a week for couples (2009–10).

It is possible to receive either component of Pension Credit exclusively or a combination of both.

> **Carmella** is 61 years old, single and has no savings. Her basic State Pension is £90.70 a week. She also receives a private pension of £22 a week. Her total weekly income is therefore £112.70. By claiming Pension Credit, she can boost her weekly income by £17.30 a week – that is:
>
> £130.00 − (£90.70 + £22) = £17.30

From 2010, the age from which you can get Pension Credit will gradually increase in line with increases to the State Pension age.

The Pension Service offers an online calculator that can help you to work out your potential entitlement to Pension Credit. But it does not cover every circumstance, so you should treat it only as a guide. You will find the calculator at www.direct.gov.uk/

Claiming Pension Credit

You can make an application for Pension Credit by ringing the Pension Credit application line on 0800 99 1234. Lines are open Monday to Friday, 8.00am to 8.00pm.

What am I entitled to if my partner dies?

Bereavement Allowance

To qualify for **Bereavement Allowance**, you need to be aged between 45 and State Pension age when your spouse or civil partner dies, and must not be bringing up children. Your spouse or civil partner must also have paid sufficient NI, or his or her death must have been caused by his or her job (that is, a work-related accident).

The full standard rate of £95.25 a week (2009–10) is payable if you are over 55 years old. If you are aged between 45 and 54, you will get a percentage of this rate (see below).

Age-related Bereavement Allowance (2009–10)				
Age	45	46	47	48	49
Rate	£28.58	£35.24	£41.91	£48.58	£55.25
Age	50	51	52	53	54
Rate	£61.91	£68.58	£75.25	£81.92	£88.58

Payments are taxable and paid for a maximum of 52 weeks, but they stop if you:

- remarry;
- form a civil partnership;
- live with someone as though you were married or civil partners; or
- reach State Pension age.

Bereavement Payment

Bereavement Payment is a one-off, tax-free lump sum of £2,000. To qualify for this payment, your spouse or civil partner must have paid at least 25 weeks' NI in any one tax year.

It is normally paid only to people who are under State Pension age, but if you are over State Pension age, you may still qualify if your spouse or civil partner did not qualify for a State Pension.

Widowed Parent's Allowance

Widowed Parent's Allowance is a taxable benefit for widows or widowers who are under State Pension age and who are entitled to Child Benefit. To qualify for this benefit, your spouse or civil partner must have paid at least one qualifying year's NI contribution. The maximum rate is paid if your spouse or civil partner had paid NI contributions for 90 per cent of his or her working life.

For more information on bereavement payments, visit www.jobcentreplus.gov.uk

Improving your basic State Pension

If you have reached, or when you reach, State Pension age, you can use your deceased spouse's or civil partner's NI contribution record if it gives you a better State Pension than one based on your own NI record. (This is the Category B pension, discussed above at page 6–7.) But you cannot do this if:

- you have remarried; or
- you are receiving a bereavement benefit.

If you are receiving Widowed Parent's Allowance when you reach State Pension age, you may be able to claim a basic State Pension at the same rate. But this cannot exceed the maximum basic State Pension payable to an individual when added to any entitlement based on your own NI record.

Additional State Pension for a widowed person

If you are over State Pension age and widowed, and as long as your spouse or civil partner had built up entitlement to additional State Pension, you will be able to inherit – that is, to claim – a share of it. The amount that you will inherit is between 50 per cent and 100 per cent of your spouse's or civil partner's additional State Pension, depending on the year in which he or she was born.

Summary

There are currently two tiers of State Pension:

- the flat-rate basic State Pension; and
- the earnings-related additional State Pension.

The State Pension is payable from the time at which you reach State Pension age – but remember that the State Pension age is changing for both men and women. How this will affect you will depend on your date of birth. How much State Pension you receive will therefore depend on when you reach State Pension age, the number of qualifying years that you have accumulated your personal NI contribution history and your earnings.

You will no doubt have a number of decisions to make in relation to your State Pension, such as whether or not to pay a voluntary contribution, and whether or not to defer claiming it. Like all things, before making decisions, it is important that you gather as much information as you can. Your starting point should be getting a State Pension forecast.

2
Pensions at work

Different types of work pension

In this chapter, we will look at the different types of work pension that are available.

Although it is not currently compulsory for employers to offer their staff membership of a pension scheme, many of them do so. If the firm for which you work employs five or more people, it should, as a minimum, offer you access to a stakeholder plan (see Chapter 3). Your employer is not, however, required to contribute to the scheme.

If your employer does offer the chance to join a pension scheme, the benefits can form a significant part of your remuneration package. Not only will your employer be paying a contribution towards your pension, but your contribution will also receive tax relief.

 Contributions to an occupational scheme are taken from your pay before tax is deducted (but not before National Insurance (NI) contributions are made). You therefore pay tax only on what is left.

Schemes that are set up by employers are run by a board of trustees and are known as occupational pension schemes. (Schemes that the government has set up for public-sector workers are also known as occupational pension schemes.)

If your employer offers you an occupational pension scheme, it will be either:

- a **salary-related** scheme; or
- a **money-purchase scheme**.

We will explain both of these in this chapter.

Alternatively, it might be a mixture of these two types. Schemes that are a mixture are normally known as **hybrid** schemes and come in various forms, but all combine salary-related and money-purchase schemes in some way – usually by giving members the better of the two calculations.

*Instead of offering an occupational scheme, some employers pay contributions, on behalf of their employees, to **group personal pension** policies (including group stakeholder plans). Although easily confused with occupational schemes, these are, in reality, individual arrangements (see Chapter 3).*

Salary-related schemes

As the name suggest, salary-related schemes are based on your salary. When you retire, these schemes pay you a pension that is based on a proportion of your salary. What this proportion is varies from scheme to scheme: in some schemes, it is your full earnings; in others, it is only part of your pay that counts. Some schemes may base your pension on your salary near to your retirement, while others use your salary in the years approaching retirement, or even your average salary throughout your years in the scheme.

Salary-related schemes are commonly called final salary pension schemes. This term can be a bit of a misnomer, because the salary used in the calculation may not necessarily be your final salary.

These types of scheme are becoming increasingly rare. While the majority of public-sector workers still enjoy membership of a salary-related scheme, most schemes in the private sector are now closed to new members. If your employer still offers you membership of a salary-related scheme, you will have some certainty about the level of pension that you can expect to get when you retire.

Although your contributions and those that your employer makes are invested, the benefits to which you are entitled are not dependent on the rise or fall in the value of investments; instead, your benefits are based on a formula that is defined in the rules of the scheme. For that reason, you may also find that salary-related schemes are called **defined-benefit** schemes.

How much you may have to contribute to a salary-related scheme will be decided by your employer. Normally, employees contribute up to 6 per cent of their pay, but the amount may be higher. The cost of the benefits that you are building up will usually be higher than the amount that you are contributing, but your employer will be paying this additional share of the cost.

In the private sector, the level of benefit that salary-related schemes will pay is set out in rules that form part of the documentation that lays out how the scheme is run. For public-sector schemes, the benefit basis is set out by legislation.

With the exception of schemes in the public sector (because they are established by legislation), salary-related schemes are set up under trust. This means that the assets of the scheme are kept separate from those of the employer, and that trustees are appointed to make sure that the scheme is run in accordance with the scheme's rules and with pension legislation.

Contributions

The trustees invest the contributions made by employees and their employer for the long term, in order for the scheme to have enough money to afford to meet all of its pension promises.

Benefits at retirement

In a salary-related scheme, the pension that you receive is based upon:

- the number of years for which you have been a member of the scheme (known as your **pensionable service**);

- the salary used by your scheme prior to your retirement or the date on which you left the company (known as your final **pensionable salary**); and

• the proportion of those earnings that your pension scheme gives you for each year of your membership (often called the **accrual rate**).

The most common accrual rates are 1/60th or 1/80th of a member's pensionable earnings for each year of pensionable service.

> **Brenda** has been a member of her company final salary scheme for 20 years. The scheme gives pension benefits based on 1/60th of pensionable salary for each year of service. Her pensionable salary is £15,000. The pension she has built up is therefore:
>
> $$\frac{£15,000}{60} \times 20 \text{ years} = £5,000 \text{ a year}$$

Most salary-related schemes will offer members the option of receiving a smaller pension in exchange for a tax-free cash lump sum. Like the calculation of a pension (as in the example above), in a salary-related scheme, the amount of cash that you can receive will depend on the length of time for which you were a member of the plan. How much pension you need to give up in exchange for the cash sum will depend upon the rules of your particular pension scheme.

A common basis on which to calculate the lump sum is 1/80th of final pensionable salary for each year of pensionable service, multiplied by three.

Brenda's tax-free cash sum would be calculated as:

$$\frac{£15,000}{80} \times 20 \text{ years} \times 3 = £11,250 \text{ a year}$$

The amount of pension that Brenda is required to give up so that she can receive this cash sum will depend upon the rules of her scheme.

When can I retire?

When you are able to retire will depend on your scheme's rules. Most salary-related schemes have a normal retirement age of between 60 and 65.

If you are over 55 years old (50 years old until 6 April 2010), some schemes may allow you to retire early. This is normally subject to the agreement of your employer and/or the scheme's trustees. It also usually means that a lower pension is paid, to take account of the early payment date. Special rules may also apply if you are made redundant.

If you are in ill health, some schemes will allow your pension to be paid early whatever your age. Normally, pensions paid early because of health reasons are payable on better terms than paid early due to normal early retirement. In order to retire on grounds of ill health, however, the member will normally need to demonstrate medical evidence that shows the effect that the ill health is having on his or her ability to work. He or she will also need to supply evidence that the condition is likely to persist until the scheme's normal retirement age.

Your rights to early retirement will depend on your scheme's rules. These rules will also stipulate if someone else's agreement to early retirement is required. Similarly, the scheme's rules will explain whether an ill-health pension can be paid and, if it can, the medical criteria that you will need to meet. The rules will also state who decides.

To establish your rights and options, you should make contact with your pension scheme or ask to see its rules.

What happens if I die before retiring?

If you die before reaching retirement age, most salary-related schemes will pay a pension to your spouse or civil partner. This will normally be a percentage (for example, 50 per cent) of the pension that you have built up. Some schemes will also pay a pension for children and it is also common for a refund to be paid of any contributions that you may have made.

Some schemes now treat a cohabiting partner in a stable relationship in the same way as they would a spouse or civil partner. Where this is the case, some schemes will require you (and possibly your partner) to complete a declaration form to confirm your relationship.

Check what the rules of your scheme say about whether it will pay a pension to a cohabiting partner in the same way as it would a spouse or civil partner.

Death in service

Additionally, as a by-product of joining, membership of many salary-related schemes means that members also enjoy rights to **death-in-service** cover. This is similar to a life assurance policy. If your scheme provides death-in-service cover, a lump sum can be paid to a beneficiary on your death. The value of the lump sum is normally calculated as a multiple of your final earnings. The lump sum can be paid free of tax as long as it is less than your available **lifetime allowance** (see Chapter 7).

The scheme's trustees decide to whom the death-in-service lump sum is paid. In this way, the trustees can make sure that your circumstances at the time of your death are properly taken into account. It also means that the payment avoids any inheritance tax (IHT) complications. (Because the payment is made via trust, there is no IHT issue, whatever the size of the payment.)

While the trustees have full discretion over to whom to pay the lump sum, you will be asked to complete an expression of wish form – normally when you first join the scheme – to indicate to whom you would like any lump sum to be paid in the event of your death.

Although the form is not legally binding on your scheme's trustees, it is important to keep your expression of wish form up to date, so that they are aware of your wishes – for example, if your relationships or personal circumstances change.

The exact level of benefit payable (including pension and death-in-service cover) will depend on the rules of your pension scheme. To clarify the level of benefit that your scheme will pay, you should ask your pensions manager for details. Check it out now to ensure that your family would be properly provided for if you were to die.

What happens if I leave the scheme before retirement age?

As long as you have been a member of the scheme for at least two years, you will be entitled to be paid a pension when you reach your scheme's retirement age. Between your leaving date and your retirement, your pension will be increased to take account of price inflation. Even after you leave, some schemes will pay benefits if you die before reaching retirement age.

If you have been a member for more than three months and are more than one year from the scheme's normal retirement age, you will also have the option of arranging for the value of the pension that you have built up (known as a **transfer value**) to be paid to another pension plan. By doing so, you will be giving up your pension rights in your old scheme and buying further pension rights in your new scheme. The amount of extra benefit to which you may be entitled will depend on the type of scheme that you have now joined.

You should consider getting financial advice before you decide to transfer a pension plan, to make sure that doing so is in your best interests (see Chapter 6).

If you have been a member of the scheme for less than two years, some schemes will – subject to certain deductions – offer you the option of taking a refund of what you have contributed. This does not include what your employer paid in.

Money-purchase schemes

In money-purchase schemes, your contributions and those made by your employer are paid into an investment fund – often invested in the stock market – in the hope that the investment will attract a positive rate of return. When you retire, your fund is used to give you an income. Because the rate of contribution – rather than how the pension is calculated – is defined in their rules, money-purchase schemes are sometimes called **defined-contribution** schemes.

The value of your fund will rise and fall depending on how much you can afford to save and how well your investments perform. The cost of buying an annuity with your pension fund can also change. Because of this, you will not know the amount of pension that you will receive at retirement until the date on which you retire.

Contributions

The scheme's rules will set out how much you have to contribute, but some schemes will allow you some choice in relation to the level of contribution that you pay. Your employer will also normally contribute, but this may depend on the level of your own contributions. For example, some employers will match their employee's contributions – but usually only up to a set limit.

> **Rashida** pays 7 per cent of her salary into her pension scheme. Her employer matches her contribution, but only up to a maximum of 6 per cent. The total contribution made into Rashida's pension plan is therefore 13 per cent of her salary.

The contributions that you make and those made on your behalf are invested in a fund, and used exclusively to provide benefits for you when you retire.

Benefits at retirement

At retirement, you can take up to 25 per cent of your fund as a tax-free lump sum. The rest of your fund must be used to provide an income. This is usually done by purchasing an **annuity** or, more rarely, by using an **unsecured pension** arrangement, which, in turn, provides you with a regular income in your retirement (see Chapter 5).

The amount of money in your fund will depend on:

- how much you (and your employer) have paid into the scheme;
- how well your investments have performed; and
- the cost of buying an income when you retire.

In most money-purchase schemes, when you retire, the trustees will use your fund to buy you an annuity with an insurance company (see Chapter 5).

Check that the annuity that the trustees are offering you is the best value. You will have the right to shop around and you may be able to get a better deal elsewhere.

When can I retire?

Your scheme's rules will include a normal retirement age – usually, between the ages of 60 and 65.

It is normally possible to retire from the age of 55 (50 until 6 April 2010), but the earlier you retire, the less the time for which your pension fund will have been invested. It will therefore have had a shorter time in which to grow, and the younger you are, the more expensive the cost of buying an annuity will be. Additionally, depending on the type of investment that you have chosen, using your fund earlier than the scheme's normal retirement age may mean that a lower amount is paid.

What happens if I die before retiring?

In the event of your death before retirement, your pension scheme may use the value of your pension fund to purchase an annuity for your dependant(s). Alternatively, it may pay a refund of the fund that you have built up.

The types of benefit will vary from scheme to scheme. Ask your scheme manager for the rules on what would happen if you were to die before retirement. It is best that you look into it now, to ensure that your family would be properly provided for in the event of your death.

Death in service

As a by-product of membership of many money-purchase schemes, you may enjoy the right to death-in-service cover. This is similar to a life assurance policy.

If your scheme provides death-in-service cover, a lump sum can be paid to a beneficiary on your death. The value of the lump sum is normally calculated as a multiple of your final earnings. The lump sum can be paid free of tax as long as it is less than your available lifetime allowance (see Chapter 7). But the payment of such a lump sum is subject to the discretionary decision of your scheme's trustees.

While the trustees have full discretion over to whom the payment should be made, you will be asked to complete an expression of wish form – normally when you first join the scheme – to indicate to whom you would prefer any money to be paid. Although the form is not legally binding on your scheme's trustees, it is important to keep your expression of wish form up to date, so that they are aware of your wishes – for example, if your relationships or personal circumstances change.

What happens if I leave the scheme before retirement age?

If you leave the scheme before your retirement age, although you will no longer be able to contribute to the scheme, your fund will remain invested and you will hopefully benefit from any future investment growth. Alternatively, you can arrange for a transfer value to be paid to another pension plan. But the amount transferred may not always represent the actual value of your fund. This will depend on the type of investment fund that the trustees of the pension were using.

For example, some funds build up through the award of annual bonuses, but the amount is only guaranteed if you retire on the date that you originally selected. If you transfer, or retire earlier than that date, depending on investment conditions at the time, your pension provider may have the right to reduce your fund by something that is normally called a **market value reduction (MVR)**.

You should consider getting financial advice before you decide to transfer, to make sure that transferring is in your best interests (see Chapter 6).

Boosting your pension

If you want to boost your retirement saving, one way of doing so will be through an **additional voluntary contribution (AVC)** scheme. Many occupational pension schemes offer their members the ability to make extra savings via AVC arrangements.

AVC arrangements either boost your pension by allowing you to buy additional pensionable service (often called **added years**), or operate on a money-purchase basis, which means that, on your retirement, the fund generated by your extra savings is used to buy extra pension, boost your cash sum, or both. Both possibilities are explained below.

Contributions to AVC arrangements enjoy the same tax concessions as contributions to your main scheme. You can use the proceeds of AVC arrangements to bridge any gaps in your pension saving caused by breaks in service or early retirement, for example.

Added years

The option of buying added years is only a possibility for members of salary-related schemes. If your scheme allows you to buy added years, this will allow you to increase the number of years of service on the basis of which your pension benefits are finally calculated. The extra added years that you have bought will boost both the amount of pension that you will receive and your tax-free cash sum, irrespective of when you started contributing.

How much you pay for added years will be worked out by your pension scheme. The cost will depend on how many years you want to buy and other factors, such as your age and your salary.

You can normally pay for added years either by means of a one-off lump sum or by making regular payments.

Money-purchase AVCs

Under a money-purchase AVC arrangement, your extra contributions are invested – usually with an insurance company – to build up a pension fund. The fund is then used to buy extra pension or, if the scheme allows, to improve your tax-free cash sum when you retire. Consequently, the amount of extra benefit that you will receive will depend on:

- how much extra you are able to save;
- the returns achieved by your investments; and
- the cost of buying a pension when you retire.

It is common for employers to bear some, or all, of the cost of running an AVC scheme and some schemes also offer special terms when the fund is finally used to buy benefits – for example, they may give better terms than those generally available in the market.

Alternatives to AVCs

It used to be the case that the number of pension plans to which you could contribute at the same time was restricted. Since April 2006, however, all such restrictions have been lifted. At the same time, occupational schemes no longer have to offer an AVC option.

Consequently, in addition – or as an alternative – to AVCs, individuals can also make extra savings for retirement through individual pension plans, such as personal pensions or stakeholder policies (see Chapter 3).

Are there limits on the extra contributions that I can make?

As well as the limits on the number of schemes into which you can pay at any one time, from April 2006, the limit on the amount of contribution that you can make was also lifted; instead, annual and lifetime allowances were introduced. These limit how much you can pay and still get tax relief (see Chapter 7).

Some AVC schemes have, however, kept limits on the amount of extra contributions that you can make to them.

 You should check with your scheme what limits, if any, apply.

Are work pensions safe?

Salary-related schemes

If your employer were to choose to close your pension scheme, it would continue to have a responsibility to fund the scheme sufficiently so that benefits built up to the date of closure were still paid when they became due.

If, however, your employer were to become insolvent, it is possible that there would not be enough money in your scheme to pay for all of the pension commitments. If that were to happen, help may be available from the Pensions Protection Fund (PPF).

The PPF was set up to help members of occupational **salary-related pension schemes** whose employers became insolvent after 6 April 2005. As long as certain conditions are met, the PPF will take over the scheme and pay regular compensation to the scheme's members.

The level of compensation differs depending upon whether you are over or under your scheme's retirement age when your company becomes insolvent.

If you are over your scheme's normal retirement age, or if you retired early because

of ill health, the PPF aims to provide 100 per cent of benefits.

If you are below the normal pension age, compensation is limited to 90 per cent of your benefits, subject to a cap. The 2009–10 cap is equivalent to £28,742.69 at the age of 65. A proportionally lower cap applies for anyone below the age of 65.

Company mergers and takeovers

The way in which companies merge or are taken over by other companies can, unsurprisingly, cause employees to worry about their pension arrangements. But, broadly speaking, the rights that you built up to the date of any change of employer should be unaffected by such corporate transactions.

If your employment is transferred and you are subject to requirements under the Transfer of Undertakings (Protection of Employment) Regulations 2006 (known as TUPE), your new employer must offer you either a salary-related scheme (which has to meet a minimum benefit test) or a money-purchase scheme (under which it matches your contributions to at least 6 per cent).

If a corporate transaction resulted in the transfer of pension rights to another scheme, before a transfer of your pension rights could take place, the scheme must either have received your consent or obtained a certificate from an actuary that confirms that your built-up benefits will be no less favourable after the transfer.

Money-purchase schemes

Money-purchase schemes are not protected by the PPF – but if you contribute to a money-purchase scheme and your employer becomes insolvent, you should bear in mind that the money in your pension fund is held completely separately from your employer's assets. You will remain entitled to the level of benefit that your fund can afford, and the value of your fund will continue to rise and fall with the value of the investments.

The security of your pension fund will depend on where it is invested. The value of your fund is subject to the performance of your chosen investment and there is no protection against your investment falling in value.

Protection may be available should the financial firm providing your investment fund(s) become insolvent. If that happens, the Financial Services Compensation Scheme (FSCS) may provide help. The FSCS has different levels of protection depending on the type of investment.

 For more information on the FSCS, visit www.fscs.org.uk

Finding old pensions

Over your working life, it is quite likely that you will change jobs and change pension schemes. Companies also change hands and the administrators of your former pension schemes may change. You may even forget to tell your former schemes about your address changes. All of this can mean that, when you retire, your former scheme(s) may not be able to trace you or you may not be able to find them.

 Keep in touch with your pension provider. Make sure that you let it know of changes to your address.

How can I claim my pension?

To claim your pension, you should write to the pension scheme administrators, giving details of your dates of employment, date of birth and NI number. You should enclose copies of any letters or certificates that show your entitlement to pension benefit.

What if I cannot find my pension scheme?

If you are having trouble finding your pension scheme, the Pension Tracing Service (see Chapter 10) may be able to help you. You can ask it to check the contact details that it may have for your scheme.

What else can I do?

Former colleagues may be in possession of useful information. Alternatively, Companies House (see Chapter 10) may know what happened to the company by which you were employed and this may also help with tracking down the pension scheme's administrators.

Am I due a pension?

It has not always been the case that a pension scheme had to set up a pension benefit for you if you left before retirement. Your rights to a pension will depend on your scheme's rules and when you left.

If you left your job before April 1975, you will only be entitled to a pension if the rules of your pension scheme specifically required it. Legislation at that time did not require schemes to set up pension benefits for early leavers. In most cases, if you paid into the scheme, your contributions were refunded on leaving. If you did not pay contributions, your record would simply often be cancelled.

If the scheme were to grant a pension, it would be normal for it to issue you with a certificate of entitlement when you left. If you do not have such a certificate, it will be very unlikely that you will be able to prove your claim if your former scheme has no record of you.

If you left between April 1975 and April 1988, were over the age of 26 and had been in a scheme for at least five years, new rules at that time meant that a pension should have been set up for you, for payment at your retirement age. If you left before you were 26 years old or before you had completed five years' service, it is likely that you would have received only a refund of your contributions.

For leavers after April 1988, the law changed again. Now, if you leave with more than two years service, a pension should be set up for you for payment at your scheme's retirement age. If you left with less than two years' service and do not have a notice of entitlement, it is likely that you were paid a refund of any contributions that you made.

It is important, therefore, that you keep safe any documentation that proves your entitlement to a pension.

Small pensions

By paying into a pension scheme, the government gives away relatively generous tax relief. But, as a result, it limits when you can draw benefits and in what form. In particular, the level of cash that you can receive is normally limited to 25 per cent of the value of your benefits.

If a pension is relatively small, you may prefer to receive a cash sum instead of a pension. But you can only give up your right to a pension, entirely for cash, if certain criteria are met.

To be able to be paid a cash sum in lieu of your entire pension, you must:

- be over the age of 60 and under the age of 75; and
- have pension plans that total in value no more than £17,500 (2009–10).

How your pension plans are valued depends on the type of scheme into which you have paid.

For money-purchase schemes, the value used is the market value of your fund(s).

For salary-related schemes, a factor of 20:1 is used. For example, if you are entitled to a pension of £1,000 a year, its value will be calculated as:

£1,000 x 20 = £20,000

In addition to the rules above, legislation that took effect on 1 June 2009 means that, from

1 December 2009, occupational pension schemes are allowed to offer members a cash sum in exchange for their pension if their pension is worth less than £2,000. If you think that this may apply to you, you should check with your scheme to see whether it will make such a payment.

The 2012 plans for auto-enrolment

As part of its objective to improve retirement saving, the government will, in the future, be making it a requirement that all employees are automatically enrolled into pension schemes. It is expected that this requirement will take effect from 2012.

Under the plans, all employees aged 22 and older, and who are earning more than a minimum amount (£5,035 a year when the plans were outlined in 2006–07), will need to be enrolled into a qualifying workplace pension scheme. If the employer does not offer such a scheme, it can use a new national pension scheme that, for now, is being called **personal accounts**.

A qualifying workplace pension scheme will be either a money-purchase scheme into which the employer pays at least 3 per cent of qualifying earnings, or a salary-related scheme that meets a minimum benefit test.

Employees will be given the chance to opt out of their employer's pension scheme or personal account, but if they remain in the scheme, a minimum level of contribution must be paid by both the employee and the employer, as follows.

- Employees will have to contribute 4 per cent of qualifying earnings.
- Employers will have to pay a minimum contribution of 3 per cent of qualifying earnings.
- The State will pay 1 per cent, in the form of tax relief.

Qualifying earnings were between £5,035 and £33,540 (when the plans were outlined in 2006–07).

Personal accounts

From 2012, employers who do not offer their staff a suitable work-based pension scheme will have to enrol their employees into a personal account. Personal accounts will be a money-purchase type of pension scheme. Contributions to the scheme will be in line with the levels noted above, although both employers and employees can pay more if they want to do so. There will, however, be an overall limit on the total amount that can be paid each year. When the plans were outlined in 2006–07, this limit was set at £3,600.

Personal accounts will be independent of the government and run by a board of trustees. The self-employed will also be allowed to pay into personal accounts.

Summary

Pension schemes offered by employers are either salary-related or money-purchase schemes. It is important to find out as much as you can about the scheme that you are in, so that you understand the benefits to which you are – and will be – entitled.

Keep in touch with your scheme and keep safe any documentation that you have received that sets out your entitlement to benefits.

Presently, employers do not have to offer their staff the chance to join a pension scheme – but changes due in 2012 will mean that all employees need to be automatically enrolled into a good work-based pension plan.

3
Going it alone

If your employer does not have its own pension arrangement or if you are self-employed, you can use a private individual plan to save for your retirement.

Even if your employer does run its own scheme and you have joined the scheme, you can still make extra savings into your own plan as well.

A private individual pension plan is a long-term savings policy that is solely designed to give you an income in retirement. You can take one out via an insurance company, bank or building society.

Stakeholder pensions, personal pension plans and **self-invested personal pensions (SIPP)** are all types of private individual plan. They are all money-purchase schemes (see Chapter 2). Money-purchase schemes build up a pension fund using your contributions (and any made by your employer), the tax relief on your contributions and investment growth. When you retire, some of the fund can be used to pay you a lump sum and the rest will be used to give you an income.

While these types of personal pension plan are very similar, there are some notable differences.

Stakeholder pensions

Stakeholder pensions must have certain features, as follows.

- During the first ten years for which you have the plan, the annual charges made for managing it cannot be more than 1.5 per cent of the value of the fund. After that time, charges must drop to no more than 1 per cent.
- The minimum contribution for which the plan provider asks cannot be more than £20.
- You must be allowed to vary or suspend your contribution without incurring extra charges.
- Transfers from a stakeholder to another pension plan should be penalty-free.
- If you do not want to choose an investment fund, the stakeholder provider must have a default fund into which your contributions can be paid.

Personal pensions

While there is no specific limit on the charges that can be made for personal pensions, the charges are often similar to those for stakeholder pensions. They can sometimes be higher than those for stakeholder plans, but a personal pension normally offers more choice in relation to where you can invest your contributions.

Self-invested personal pensions (SIPPs)

SIPPs are a type of personal pension that allow savers much greater freedom in relation to where they can invest. As well as investing in funds run by insurance companies and financial companies, contributions to a SIPP can also be used to own investments directly, such as **shares** and commercial property. They are therefore normally seen as appropriate for people who understand investments. They usually also have higher charges than stakeholders and personal pensions.

While you have a greater choice in relation to where you can invest, you do need to bear in mind that the investment decisions will be yours. You therefore need to make sure that you have the time to do the research and to keep an eye on your investments. And remember: if your investments go wrong, you'll have no one else to blame.

Individual arrangements set up by employers

Some employers make individual pension plans available into which their employees can pay. Pension plans arranged this way are known as group personal pensions (GPPs), group stakeholder pensions or group SIPPs, depending on the type of pension plan that the employer has set up.

While easily confused with occupational schemes, these are really individual plans – but ones for which the employer has chosen the scheme provider. The employer may have negotiated with the scheme provider for reduced charges for its employees.

If your employer has five or more employees, it must allow you to pay into a stakeholder plan if it has neither an occupational scheme nor a suitable GPP that you can join. Your employer does not have to pay into a stakeholder plan, but if it offers you a GPP or a group SIPP as an alternative to a stakeholder pension, it must pay a contribution that is equal to at least 3 per cent of your basic salary.

Once the rules on auto-enrolment take effect (see Chapter 2), the requirement for employers to give access to a stakeholder pension will end.

Because these types of scheme are really individual arrangements, if you leave your employer, you will be able to continue to pay contributions into your pension. Any contribution that your former employer made will stop, however, and you may have to pay higher annual administration charges.

Instead of offering an occupational scheme, some employers pay contributions on behalf of their employees to group personal pension policies (including group stakeholder plans). Although easily confused with occupational schemes, these are, in reality, individual arrangements. Occupational schemes are either set up under a trust or by legislation. Group personal pensions and group stakeholder plans are set up through a contract between the pension provider and the policyholder.

Contributions

These days, you can pay as much as you like into a private pension plan, but how much tax relief you get on your contributions is limited. Tax relief is limited to contributions of up to 100 per cent of your annual earnings or a limit known as the **annual allowance** (£245,000 in 2009–10), whichever is the lower figure.

There is also a lifetime allowance, which limits how much you can build up in all of your pension funds (£1.75 million in 2009–10). If you are lucky enough to have total pension savings worth more than the lifetime allowance, a tax charge will be made against the surplus when you draw your benefits (see Chapter 7).

As long as you are not putting more into the scheme than the annual limits above, basic rate tax relief is added to the contributions that you make. This means that, for every £100 that you want put into your plan, you only have to pay £80.

If you are a higher rate taxpayer, you can claim further tax relief via your tax return.

Even if you are a non-taxpayer, you can still get tax relief on your contributions – but only up to a gross contribution limit of £3,600. This means that you can pay £2,880, which, when tax relief is added, is worth £3,600. You can pay more, but any extra contributions will not attract tax relief.

If your employer also pays into your plan, these contributions will not attract any tax relief for you.

Investing your money

A private pension is a money-purchase scheme. This means that your contributions are paid into an investment fund – often invested in the stock market – in the hope that the investment will attract a positive rate of return.

If you are paying into a personal pension or a stakeholder plan, your pension provider will offer you a range of investment funds from which to choose. With a stakeholder plan, you do not have to make a choice, because all stakeholder providers must offer a default fund into which savers can pay.

Some providers may limit how many different funds you can select and/or how often you can switch to a different fund.

 Check the choice that your pension provider offers and how often it will let you switch investments, along with what charges, if any, apply.

If you are paying into a SIPP, you will have a much greater choice in relation to in what you can invest. Your pension plan will be able to own the investments directly – for example, your SIPP can own individual company shares or commercial property. You will also have control over the investment strategy or be able to appoint a fund manager to manage your investments for you.

There are various types of investment and what suits you will depend upon the level of risk that you are prepared to take. Investments that carry the most risk, such as shares, have the potential to produce the best returns over the long term. But selecting investments that are described as relatively safe, or less risky, does not mean that they have no risk. While such investments may not be as potentially volatile as shares, low returns may mean that the value of your savings will not keep up with inflation.

While you cannot avoid risk completely, spreading your investments across the main investment classes is one way of trying to find the right balance. The old saying 'Don't put all your eggs in one basket' is one way in which to summarise this strategy.

If you are some way from retirement, you may want to choose funds that have the long-term potential to give the best results. But if your retirement is near (that is, between ten and five years away), you may want to think about funds that are more stable – even though they may not necessarily have the potential to produce the best returns. This is because values can go down as well as up and, if you are trying to plan your forthcoming retirement, it may be easier for you to plan for stability than to chase potentially high returns.

The range of funds offered by pension providers does vary – but the choices that you will be given will be likely to include saving in funds that invest in the following types of investment.

Cash

Investing in cash means that you put your money into deposit accounts, such as those run by banks or building societies.

Cash is considered a safe option, but the rate of return that it offers is unlikely to be attractive. It will not normally be suitable for people who are saving for the long term.

Bonds

Bonds are loans made by investors to the government, local authorities or companies. In return, the investor receives interest and, at the end of the term, it is expected that his or her loan is repaid.

Historically, bonds have produced better returns than cash, but lower returns than shares.

The main risk relating to bonds is that a loan will not be repaid. This is, however, unlikely in relation to loans to governments.

Shares (equities)

By investing in share funds, you are investing in private companies. Companies issue shares in their businesses, known as **equities**, and these are bought and sold on the stock market. As the value of a company increases, so does the value of its shares.

Historically, such investments have produced the best returns – but they also carry greater risk. Over the short term, the value of shares can go up or down dramatically.

Property

Property funds invest in commercial properties, such as offices, shops and factories. The value of units in these funds is linked to the rents received from the tenants and the value of the properties held by the fund. Pension schemes cannot invest in residential property.

Historically, property has produced better returns than bonds and cash, but lower returns than shares.

Mixed funds

Some funds offered will be a mixture of the above investment types. Common types of mixed fund are as follows.

With-profits funds

The money invested in with-profits funds is spread among a mix of investment types, such as shares, bonds, property and cash. Investors buy units in the fund and, depending on how well the underlying investments perform, they receive bonuses, which are added to their funds.

The value of the original units bought is guaranteed and some plans also have guarantees on the rate of bonuses paid. Once bonuses are paid, they cannot normally be taken away.

When calculating the bonus, the company usually tries to balance performance over the long term by holding back some of the gains in the good years to pay out in poor years. This is called smoothing returns.

Managed funds

Managed funds are made up of a mixture of different types of investment. Spreading investment over a mixture of different types in this way reduces investment risk.

Lifestyle funds

The principle behind lifestyle funds is that while the investor is some time away from retirement, his or her contributions are invested mainly, or entirely, in shares. As the investor approaches retirement, those funds are gradually switched into safer investments, such as bonds and cash.

Switching usually takes place between five and ten years from your chosen retirement age.

 Consider your own attitude to risk, taking into account the length of time for which you will be saving. If you are at all uncertain, you should consider obtaining independent financial advice (see Chapter 6).

Benefits at retirement

When you retire, you can take up to 25 per cent of your fund as a tax-free lump sum; the balance will be used to give you an income.

You will not know the amounts of lump sum and income that will be paid until the date on which you retire. Those amounts will depend on:

- how much you have been able to save;
- how well your investments have performed; and
- the cost of paying you an income when you retire.

You can convert your fund into income in two ways:

- by buying an annuity; or
- by setting up an income drawdown arrangement.

Each of these options is discussed in Chapter 5.

When can I retire?

You can use your pension plan to pay benefits at any age between the ages of 55 (50, until 6 April 2010) and 75. If you are in ill health, you may be able to use your funds earlier than the age of 55, if your pension provider is satisfied that your health is such that it will permanently impact upon your ability to work. The actual criteria that you will need to meet should be explained in your plan's terms and conditions.

While it is possible to retire at any age between 55 and 75, at the outset of the plan, you will normally be asked when you intend to retire.

If you have invested in a with-profits fund, retiring at a date other than that which you originally chose when your plan was set up could mean that the value of your fund is reduced. If you are retiring at a time when investment performance is poor, the provider may apply a market value reduction (MVR) to ensure that you do not take out more than your fair share.

The MVR reflects the fact that with-profits funds pay returns over the lifetime of the plan by adding bonuses to your fund. Once added, these bonuses are normally guaranteed. The bonuses are worked out based upon past and expected future investment returns – but the underlying investments backing the fund will vary according to investment conditions. When investment performance is poor, the real value of the fund will be less than its notional value.

Because of this possibility, the pension provider normally has the right to apply an MVR if the policy is transferred or used to pay benefits at a time other than the originally selected retirement date. Normally, policies do not allow an MVR to be applied if you use your fund to pay benefits at your selected retirement age.

If you are thinking about retiring on a date other than that which you originally chose, check your policy terms to see whether or not your pension provider can apply an MVR.

Some policies include rights to valuable guarantees, such as the rate to be used when you convert the fund into an annuity on retirement. But such guarantees are often only available if you retire at your originally selected retirement age. It may also be necessary for you to choose an annuity of a certain type.

Check your policy terms to see whether your pension plan gives you rights to certain guarantees and the circumstances in which they are available.

What happens if I die before retiring?

If you die before retiring, the value of your fund can be paid as a lump sum. If the amount paid is greater than the lifetime allowance (see Chapter 7), the surplus is taxed at 55 per cent.

The decision regarding to whom the lump sum is paid is normally entirely at the discretion of your provider. When you start a plan, you will be asked to complete an expression of wish form indicating whom you would like to be considered.

Although the expression of wish form is not legally binding, it is important to keep it up to date, so that your provider is aware of your wishes. Keep it under review – especially if your relationships or personal circumstances change.

Death benefits do not have to be taken as lump sums; all, or part, of your fund can be used to provide dependants pensions.

If you have used your policy to contract out (see Chapter 4), you are married or in a civil partnership and you die before retirement, the **protected rights** fund that you have built up currently has to be used to buy a pension for your spouse or civil partner. It is, however, proposed that this requirement be removed – a change that is likely to take place in 2012.

Your plan terms should set out how your fund will be used if you die before retiring. Check the policy terms of your plan to ensure that your family is properly

*provided for in the event of your death.
Some old-style insurance policies may
pay out nothing on death.*

What happens if I stop contributing?

If you stop contributing, your fund will remain
invested and you will hopefully benefit from any
future investment growth. The value of your fund
is, however, directly linked to the value of the
investments that you have made: if the
investments fall in value, the value of your
fund will also fall.

You should also remember that even though
you are not contributing, your pension provider
will still be making charges for managing your
plan.

*In some individual pension plans, the
charge made by your provider can go up
if you stop contributing. Extra charges
such as this cannot be made, however, if
your plan is a stakeholder pension.
Check what your policy says about
charges.*

Small pots

By paying into a pension scheme, the
government gives away relatively generous tax
relief – but, as a result, it limits when you can
draw benefits and in what form. If a pension fund
is relatively small, you may prefer to receive your
entire fund as a cash sum rather than to use it to
provide an income. This type of payment is
known as a **triviality lump sum**.

It is, however, only possible to do so if certain criteria are met. You can only be paid your entire fund as a cash sum if:

- you are over the age of 60 and under the age of 75; and
- the total value of all of your pension plans is no greater than a certain amount (£17,500 in 2009–10).

How pension plans are valued depends on the type of scheme. For money-purchase schemes, such as personal pensions, the value used is the market value of your fund(s). If, however, you also have entitlement to a pension from a salary-related scheme, a factor of 20:1 is used. For example, if you are entitled to a pension of £1,000 a year, its value will be calculated as:

£1,000 x 20 = £20,000

If you can be paid your fund entirely as cash, 25 per cent of the sum will be paid tax-free, but the balance will be taxed as income.

If you are unable to receive your entire pension fund as a cash sum, then the bulk of it will need to be used to pay an income. But some companies are not interested in offering annuities in exchange for small funds – so consolidating a number of funds (see below) may be one way in which to avoid this problem.

Jenny has two pension schemes: a personal pension worth £3,500 and a salary-related scheme run by an old employer, which is due to pay a pension of £320 a year. Her salary-related pension is worth:

£320 x 20 = £6,400

Added to her personal pension pot, this means that the total value of all her pension plans is:

£3,500 + £6,400 = £9,900

It is therefore possible for Jenny to receive her benefits entirely as cash.

Consolidation

If you have a number of personal pensions, you may find bringing them together into one single plan allows you to save on management charges. When you decide to retire, you may also be able to secure a better deal when buying an annuity.

Before **consolidating**, you should compare the plans by looking at the charges that your plan providers are making and the returns that you have been receiving. You should also check if there are any exit charges or possible MVRs that will apply if you move funds, and whether you would be giving up any guarantees.

If you are at all uncertain, you should consider getting independent financial advice (see Chapter 6).

Information from your pension provider

Each year, your pension provider must send you an annual statement, which will include information on how much you have paid in and how your fund has grown during the year.

It will also forecast how much your pension could be when you retire, in terms of today's prices.

Check your statement carefully. If your contributions have not been properly recorded, it is easier to get things corrected if you act quickly after receiving your annual statement. The statement may also help you to decide whether or not you need to save more, whether or not you need to consider changing to different investment funds and whether or not to transfer to a different pension provider.

Summary

A private pension is a long-term savings plan that is designed to pay you an income when you retire. The amount that you will get at retirement will depend on:

- how much you can save;
- the level of charges taken from your fund;
- how well your investments perform; and
- the cost of providing you with an income when you retire.

It is important that you take an interest in your policy, and understand the risks and benefits involved.

4

Contracting out

Pensions are infamous for being complicated –
and among those complications, **contracting out**
is one of the issues with which people have the
most difficulty. The purpose of this chapter is to try
to explain what contracting out is all about and its
consequences.

If you are an employee, you automatically
become entitled to additional State Pension
(see Chapter 1). Contracting out allows you
to choose to opt out of the additional State
Pension. You can do this either by using
an individual pension plan or by joining a
contracted-out occupational pension scheme.
If you are contracted out, your right to a basic
State Pension is unaffected.

In broad terms, if you are contracted out, instead
of building up entitlement to the additional State
Pension, you build up replacement pension rights
in a private arrangement. You will also either pay a
lower level of National Insurance (NI), or the
government will pay part of your NI contribution
into your pension fund, depending on the type of
contracted-out pension scheme of which you are
a member.

*If you are self-employed, your NI
contribution does not qualify you for the*

additional State Pension. Contracting out is therefore not an issue for you.

Contracted-out occupational schemes

There are two types of occupational pension:

- **salary-related schemes**; or
- **money-purchase schemes**.

The way in which contracting out works differs depending on the type of scheme of which you are a member.

Salary-related schemes

When the additional State Pension was introduced in 1978 – as the **State Earnings-Related Pension Scheme** (SERPS – see Chapter 1) – it was recognised that many employees were already members of good company pension schemes. Salary-related schemes were therefore allowed to contract out of SERPS, as long as certain conditions were met.

Broadly speaking, the scheme did this by undertaking to assume the liability for its member's additional State Pension entitlement. Before 6 April 1997, schemes achieved this by allowing members to build up rights to a **Guaranteed Minimum Pension (GMP)**. The GMP more or less replicated the amount of additional State Pension to which members would otherwise have been entitled had they not been contracted out.

From 6 April 1997, the law changed and schemes no longer had to provide GMP benefits for service. Instead, to remain contracted out, a scheme had to show that the benefits for its members were, at least in broad terms, as good as certain requirements set by the government.

Members of contracted-out salary-related schemes pay NI at a lower rate (see below).

Employee National Insurance (NI) contribution rates (2009–10)	
Contracted in	0% on first £110 a week
	11% of £110.01–£844 a week
	1% on earnings above £844 a week
Contracted out (in a salary-related pension scheme)	0% on first £110 a week
	9.4% of £110.01–£770 a week
	11% of £770.01–£844 a week
	1% on earnings above £844 a week

Money–purchase schemes

From 6 April 1988, it became possible for members of money-purchase pension schemes to contract out.

If you are a member of a contracted-out occupational money-purchase scheme, both you and your employer pay NI at a lower rate – but your employer must pay into your pension fund an amount that is equal to the reduction in your and your employer's NI.

Normally, your employer will reclaim your share of this from you out of your pay. In addition, the government will also pay an extra age-related rebate of your NI directly into your pension scheme. These payments are invested and the fund that is subsequently built up is known as a protected rights fund. Other contributions that you and your employer make are invested separately.

When you eventually retire, you will use the fund that you have built up to purchase an income. If your scheme rules allow, you can also use the fund towards paying a cash sum.

Contracted-out individual plans

Individual pension plans are money-purchase schemes – but, to make things confusing, contracting out affects them differently from the way in which it affects occupational money-purchase schemes.

If you have an individual plan (for example, a personal pension or stakeholder plan), you take the decision on whether or not to contract out.

If you decide to contract out, you continue to pay NI at the full rate, but the government makes a contribution to your pension plan. This contribution consists of a rebate of part of the NI contribution that both you and your employer have paid, plus income tax relief on your share of the rebate. This contribution is invested separately from any additional contribution that you may make and the fund that is subsequently built up is described as a protected rights fund.

You can use your protected rights fund to pay retirement benefits at any time between the ages of 55 (50 until 6 April 2010) and 75. You can use 25 per cent of the fund to give you a tax-free cash sum and you will use the balance to give you an income (see Chapter 5).

Self-invested personal pensions (SIPPs – see Chapter 3) were not originally allowed to be used to contract out, but, since 1 October 2008, this rule has changed and they can now hold protected rights.

The abolition of contracting out on a money-purchase basis

Your ability to contract out using a money-purchase scheme, whether occupational or individual, will eventually be abolished. The date on which this will happen is not yet known, but it is thought that it will be from 6 April 2012.

To contract out or not to contract out

If you join a contracted-out occupational scheme, it is your employer who takes the decision to contract out. When you leave an occupational scheme, your contracted-out status will stop. But if you have an individual pension, you will be asked whether you want to contract in or out of the additional State Pension, and that choice will remain in force unless and until you make a different decision.

Choosing whether or not to contract out is difficult and the decision may not always be driven by which option is likely to give you the best retirement income.

The first thing to bear in mind is that there is no guarantee that the pension that your protected rights fund eventually purchases will be higher than the additional State Pension that you will have given up as a result of being contracted out. The eventual income that you secure may be more – but it is quite possible that it will be less. Your protected rights fund is invested, meaning that its value will depend entirely on how well that investment does.

Pension saving is a long-term investment, so your age will be a factor. As you get older, there is less investment time during which the rebates paid to your protected rights fund can grow in value. Many commentators believe that, once you reach a certain age, you should be contracted in – but the age specified will vary from adviser to adviser, and some will even suggest that there is no age at which contracting out represents good value.

Age is, however, not the only factor that you must consider. Your circumstances and attitudes to risk change over time, and there may be other factors in the future that will become more important to you than they are at present. For example, you may value the ability to take a cash sum from a protected rights fund, or you may value the fact that a contracted-out fund can be used to provide pension benefits earlier than at your State Pension age.

Whatever your decision, it is important that you review your decisions at regular intervals. And you should remember that contracting out using a money-purchase scheme is to be abolished within the next few years.

If you do decide to contract back in, you will need to ask your pension provider for form CA 1543. You should complete this and send it to HM Revenue & Customs (HMRC; see Chapter 10).

If you choose to contract back in, you can either do so from the 5 April at the end of the current tax year or backdate it to the 5 April at the end of the previous tax year.

For more guidance on contracting out, read the Financial Services Authority (FSA) guide, 'The State Second Pension (formerly SERPS) – should you be contracted out?' (see Chapter 10).

Alternatively, the Pensions Advisory Service offers online guidance about what you should consider at www.pensionsadvisoryservice.org.uk, *including an interactive web tool to help you to make your decision. You can also talk through the issues by calling its helpline on 0845 601 2923.*

Summary

In broad terms, if you are contracted out, instead of building up entitlement to the additional State Pension, you build up replacement rights in a private pension arrangement.

How the process works and what decisions you need to take will depend on the type of pension scheme that you have.

The government intends to prohibit the use of money-purchase schemes to contract out of the additional State Pension. This is likely to come into effect in 2012.

5
Annuities

If you have used a money-purchase scheme to save, to give yourself an income in retirement, you can either buy an annuity or use an unsecured pension.

- **Annuities** are sold by insurance companies. In return for your pension fund, they promise to pay you an income for the rest of your life.
- **Unsecured pensions** (also called income drawdown or income withdrawal plans) are an alternative way of receiving income, but without buying an annuity.

In this chapter, we will look at both options.

Annuities

An annuity is an insurance contract that guarantees to pay you an income for the rest of your life. Its technical name is a lifetime annuity, but for the rest of this chapter, we will use the term annuity.

How much income an annuity will pay largely depends on how big a pension fund you have been able to build up over previous years.

 If you are thinking about buying an annuity, you should ask your pension provider for an up-to-date statement of the value of your pension fund.

The rate used by insurance companies to convert your fund into an income is, however, subject to a number of factors, such as your age, gender, health and sometimes where you live. All of these will play a part in the amount of income that you will get.

- In terms of **age**, it is normally the case that the younger you are, the lower the income will be, and the older you are, the higher the income. This is because, as you get older, insurance companies expect to be paying you for a shorter period of time.
- Similarly, your **gender** will be a factor, because women are expected to live longer than men.
- **Health** and **lifestyle** can impact on your life expectancy, so these are also taken into account.
- Finally, some companies have started to take note of **where you live**, because their research suggests that this can also influence your life expectancy.

When can I buy an annuity?

You can buy an annuity at any time between the ages of 55 (50 until 6 April 2010) and 75.

If you are in ill health, you may be able to buy one earlier, as long as your pension provider is satisfied that your health is such that it will permanently affect your ability to work. The actual criteria that you will need to meet should be explained in your plan's terms and conditions.

Different types of annuity

There are a number of options available to you when choosing an annuity. The option that will suit you will depend on your personal circumstances.

The option that you choose will affect the amount of income that the annuity will pay. You can tailor your annuity to suit your needs by choosing from a range of add-ons, such as those that we outline below. Broadly speaking, however, the more add-ons that you include, the lower your starting income will be.

So, the simplest annuity – for example, one that never increases and ends on your death – will also be that which will give you a higher starting income. But while such an annuity may give you a higher starting income, in the event of your death, your spouse or partner will not receive any benefit.

Before buying an annuity, think about your personal circumstances. Do you have a partner who will rely on the income from your annuity after your death? Do you want to make sure that the value of your income keeps up with inflation? Are you in poor health?

The Pensions Advisory Service's annuity planner can help you to work your way through the decision process, online at www.pensionsadvisoryservice.org.uk

The main options, or add-ons, from which you can choose are as follows.

Single-life annuity

A **single-life annuity** will pay you an income for the rest of your life, but the income will stop on your death and no payment will be made to your spouse or partner.

Joint-life annuity

A **joint-life annuity** will pay you an income for the rest of your life, but will also pay an income (normally at a lower rate) to your spouse or partner after your death, for the rest of his or her life.

Either type can be a level annuity or an **escalating annuity**. You can also choose to have a **guarantee period**.

Level annuity

A **level annuity** will always pay the same amount of income – that is, it will not increase. While a level annuity will pay more at the outset than one that increases, if inflation rises, the value of your income will fall over time.

Escalating annuity

An escalating annuity will start at a lower rate than a level annuity, but will increase each year. Increases can be based on the **retail prices index (RPI)**, or can be a fixed amount – for example, 3 per cent or 5 per cent.

Investment-linked annuity

Like other annuities, **investment-linked** annuities will pay you an income for the rest of your life – but they do not guarantee how much they will pay, which will depend entirely on investment performance. Although this gives you the chance to receive a higher income if the value of the underlying investments rises, you also risk your income going down if the returns on the investments fall.

Guarantee period

You can choose a pension guarantee period of up to ten years (although providers usually only offer five- or ten-year options). If you die within the guarantee period, the income will continue to be paid to your spouse, civil partner or dependant until the end of the guarantee period. Alternatively, instead of receiving that income, your beneficiary can receive a lump sum that is equal in value to the remaining instalments (taxed at 35 per cent).

Brian chose a five-year pension guarantee and, sadly, died two years into payment of an annuity that paid £5,000 a year. The annuity provider gave his widow, Yvonne, the option of receiving £5,000 a year for the next three years (taxable as income) or a lump sum of £15,000 (less tax at 35 per cent).

Because Brian had chosen a joint-life annuity at 50 per cent, Yvonne also received £2,500 a year for the rest of her life.

Capital-protected annuities

Choosing a **capital-protected** (also known as a value-protected) annuity means that, if you die before reaching the age of 75, a lump sum will be payable to your estate or beneficiaries, based on the fund value that you used to buy the annuity less the income that you have been paid. The lump sum is subject to tax at 35 per cent. It may also be subject to inheritance tax (IHT) if the lump sum pushes the value of your estate over the IHT threshold when added to your other assets.

Remember, however, that capital-protected annuities are likely to be more expensive than other types of annuity and that, if you survive beyond the age of 75, you will receive no benefit for that extra cost.

Enhanced and impaired-life annuities

Some companies offer what are known as **impaired-life** annuities. These pay a level of income that is higher than normal if you have certain health problems that could affect your life expectancy.

Some companies also offer enhanced annuities, which pay a higher income if you are overweight or if you smoke.

If you suffer from poor health, check whether you could be eligible for an impaired-life annuity.

Short-term annuities

A **short-term annuity** lets you use some of your pension fund to buy an annuity that pays you an income for a fixed period of up to five years. The remainder of your fund stays invested. After the fixed period, income payments stop. Any short-term annuity must stop before you reach the age of 75.

Short-term annuities may therefore be useful if you do not want to commit all of your funds immediately – for example, because you think that annuity rates may improve in the future – but you do require some income now.

You should remember, however, that your remaining funds do remain invested, meaning that they could rise or fall, depending on investment conditions.

Do also consider that there is no guarantee that annuity rates will rise.

What happens if I die after buying an annuity?

What will happen in the event of your death after buying an annuity will depend on the type of annuity that you have bought.

If you have bought a joint-life annuity, in the event of your death, income payments will continue (normally at a lower rate) to your spouse or partner, for the rest of his or her life. The rate payable will depend on the choices that you made when the annuity was originally bought. Normally, the choice will be the same level of income, or two-thirds or a half of what you were receiving.

If the annuity that you have bought includes a guarantee period, the balance of the guarantee will still be payable if you die before the period ends.

Serious ill health

If your life expectancy is less than 12 months, you may be able to receive your fund as a cash sum, free of tax, and may therefore not need to purchase an annuity.

Shopping around

You do not have to use your pension fund to buy an annuity with your existing pension company; instead, you have the right to shop around and see whether you can get a better deal elsewhere. This is called the **open market option (OMO)** and allows you to use your pension fund to buy an annuity with a different provider.

Shopping around may mean that you get a better rate from others in the annuity market – perhaps resulting in an income that is as much as a 20 per cent higher than that offered by your pension provider.

But before shopping around, you should check what your existing provider is offering, because some pension policies include rights to valuable guarantees, such as the rate used to convert your pension fund into income.

Check with your current pension provider what it can offer and whether your policy includes guarantees, such as a guaranteed annuity rate. Check to see whether or not you will be better off by shopping around.

To help you to shop around, the Financial Services Authority (FSA) maintains a table of leading annuity providers, online at www.fsa.gov.uk/tables

By answering some basic questions, you can find out whether using the OMO is likely to benefit you. But you should bear in mind that not all annuity providers are listed on the FSA's tables and that some companies will not deal with you directly, but will require you to use a financial adviser (see Chapter 6).

Shopping around may be difficult if you have only a small pension fund. Many annuity providers have minimum funds that they will accept – typically, £5,000. If you have more than one fund, you may find that bringing them together – that is, consolidating them (see Chapter 3) – may make buying an annuity easier and could give you greater purchasing power.

Qualifying for an impaired-life or **enhanced annuity** may also make shopping around easier. Alternatively, a triviality lump sum could be an option.

It is worth shopping around to see where you can get the best deal. Get quotes from different providers for the type of annuity that you want and compare annuity prices online at the FSA site www.moneymadeclear.fsa.gov.uk

Alternatives to annuities

Unsecured pensions

It is possible to use your pension fund to pay benefits without having to buy an annuity. You can do this by means of an unsecured pension. (You may also find the terms income drawdown or income withdrawal used to describe the same thing.)

An unsecured pension lets you take up to 25 per cent of your fund as a tax-free cash sum. The balance of your fund after taking the cash sum remains invested, but can be used to pay you an income. The maximum amount of income that you can draw from your fund each year is the equivalent of 120 per cent of the amount of income that you could have got if you were to have bought a level single-life annuity instead. Your provider will work out the maximum for you, based on rates provided by the Government Actuary's Department (GAD). The maximum limit should be reviewed at least every five years. There is no minimum amount.

Because there is no minimum amount of income that has to be drawn, some people use an unsecured pension in order to obtain a cash sum to pay, for example, immediate short-term liabilities. In this way, they can leave the balance of their pension fund invested for use at a later date.

But, because your fund remains invested, you do need to be comfortable with the risk that this involves. While staying invested offers you the possibility of a higher income in the future if your investments do well, if they fail to do as well as hoped, you could find yourself worse off.

Your provider will also charge to manage your plan and these charges will be taken from your fund. If the amount of the charges (and any income that you have drawn) is more than the investment growth, the value of your fund will go down.

Benefits can be paid at any time after you reach the age of 55 (50 until 6 April 2010), but you must use the fund to buy an annuity before you reach the age of 75, or you must switch to an **alternatively secured pension** (see below). The payment of a cash sum must, however, take place within 12 months of the start of the unsecured pension.

After starting an unsecured pension, it is still possible to transfer your fund to an unsecured pension policy offered by another provider. If you are considering doing so, it will be worthwhile getting independent financial advice first (see Chapter 6).

What happens if I die while using an unsecured pension?

If you have an unsecured pension, in the event of your death, your surviving spouse, civil partner or dependant may have the option, depending on the rules of your policy, of:

- receiving a lump sum (subject to 35 per cent tax);
- drawing income using an unsecured pension (if he or she is under 75 years old);

- drawing income using an alternatively secured pension, if he or she is over the age of 75; or
- buying an annuity with the remaining funds.

Alternatively secured pensions (ASPs)

Alternatively secured pensions (ASPs) became available from 6 April 2006 and are a form of unsecured pension for people over the age of 75. They were originally intended for people who had religious objections to buying an annuity, but anyone over the age of 75 can use one.

Like an unsecured pension, you can draw an income from an ASP while keeping your fund invested. The maximum and minimum levels of income that you can draw are, however, more restrictive than an unsecured pension.

- The minimum level of income that you must draw each year is equivalent to 55 per cent of the amount that a 75-year-old could get from an annuity.
- The maximum level of income that you can draw is 90 per cent.

Both of these levels are based on rates advised by the GAD.

The risks of an ASP are similar to those of an unsecured pension. Because your fund remains invested, you need to be comfortable with the risk that this involves.

What happens if I die while using an ASP?

If you have an ASP, in the event of your death, the funds can be used to pay an income to a surviving spouse, civil partner or dependant. This can be done by buying an annuity, or using an unsecured pension (if the dependant is under the age of 75), or using another ASP (if the dependant is over the age of 75). If you have no dependants, the remaining funds can be paid to a charity that you have nominated.

If you have no dependants, the remaining funds may be paid into another arrangement that is part of the same registered pension scheme – but if this were to happen, it would attract a tax charge of up to 70 per cent.

ASPs can also have potential IHT complications. IHT would not be chargeable if, on your death, the remaining funds were to be used to benefit a dependant – but if there were to be funds remaining on the dependant's subsequent death, they would form part of the original scheme member's estate for IHT purposes.

No IHT liability will arise if funds are paid to a charity.

Summary

Buying an annuity or taking out an unsecured pension are both ways of getting an income during your retirement. What is best for you will depend on your circumstances and your attitude to risk. Before making your decision, think about your situation and with what you are comfortable.

You do not have to buy an annuity with your current pension provider. Shopping around may mean that you get a better deal elsewhere.

The Pensions Advisory Service has an online annuity planner that can help you to choose the annuity that best fits your circumstances. It offers general information and advice, and takes you step-by-step through the decision-making process for converting your pension fund into income. To access the planner, visit www.pensionsadvisoryservice.org.uk

6
Getting financial advice

You do not have to get financial advice before choosing a pension product, but if you are at all unsure about what type of plan is best for you, how much you need to save or where you should invest your money, then financial advice is a sensible thing to seek.

 Remember: *Financial advisers are not limited to advising on pensions. They can help you to make decisions about all of your money matters.*

Do you need financial advice?

If you are comfortable with making financial decisions, you may think that you do not need to seek any financial advice.

For some decisions, you may even think that the advantages of signing up are so clear that you do not need financial advice before doing so – for example, if your employer is going to pay into a pension plan on your behalf, you may recognise that not joining would be the same as giving up part of your pay.

There are also a lot of different sources from which you can get information and guidance about pensions – including, we hope, this book.

Armed with this extra knowledge, you may find yourself feeling more confident about making your pension choices.

But before making any decisions, it is worth finding out as much as you can about the options that are available to you. Think about what you have already built up, remembering to take account of your State Pension entitlement. Will this be enough for your retirement?

Get up-to-date statements from your pension providers to help you to make informed decisions.

If you want further information and guidance about different pension plans and how they work, including the State Pension, the Pensions Advisory Service will be able to help you.

The Pensions Advisory Service's website includes guidance on how to plan your saving for retirement and how to choose an annuity. There are also guides on various pension topics available online at www.pensionsadvisoryservice.org.uk

Information about pensions and other financial products can also be found at the Financial Services Authority (FSA) site www.moneymadeclear.fsa.gov.uk

Whatever you decide to do, you must make sure that you review your decisions regularly, because the value of your pensions is likely to vary and your personal circumstances may change.

If you are taking decisions yourself, try working through the 'Ten steps to building a retirement saving plan' that appear at the end of this chapter.

Who can give financial advice?

Financial advisers are regulated by the Financial Services Authority (FSA). The FSA sets certain standards that advisers must meet in order to be able to advise people about financial products.

Among the FSA's rules outlining the financial adviser's relationship with his or her customer, those relating to training and competence are particularly thorough. A person cannot give financial advice unless he or she has passed an 'appropriate qualification', such as the Certificate for Financial Advisers (CeFA®) or the Financial Planning Certificates (FPCs). There are further qualifications that a financial adviser must pass if he or she wants to give advice in certain specialist areas.

If the FSA suspects that an adviser has broken any of its rules, it has a range of powers through which it can discipline the individual (or an entire organisation). After investigation, it may limit the areas in which an individual is permitted to give advice, or it may withdraw its permission entirely. There are additional sanctions to which an adviser found guilty of misconduct may be subject, such as a financial penalty.

If you are considering getting financial advice, make sure that the firm or person with which or to whom you speak is regulated by the FSA.

 To check the FSA's register, call 0845 606 1234 or visit www.moneymadeclear.fsa.gov.uk

On what will the financial adviser base any recommendations?

The 'know your customer' rules are outlined under the Financial Services and Markets Act 2000, and require that a financial adviser takes account of your personal circumstances and aspirations, in order to recommend products that he or she believes will best suit you.

To understand your needs, a financial adviser will complete what is known as a fact find. This involves collecting a range of information about you that will help the adviser to recommend a course of action for you to follow.

Based on that fact find, the adviser will then give you a recommendation letter, explaining why he or she thinks that a particular product or firm will suit you.

He or she should also issue you with a 'Key Features' document, which will set out:

• the aim of the product(s) that he or she is recommending;

- how your payments will be invested;
- what the risks are; and
- the tax position.

The adviser should explain any charges and how they will affect your investment.

An adviser will also give you information about the firm for which he or she works. This will explain his or her service and the costs of the advice.

Take time to read these documents, so that you understand why a particular product is being recommended. Ask questions about anything that you do not understand.

Do all financial advisers work in the same way?

Not all financial advisers work in the same way: some will specialise in certain areas of finance – for example, retirement saving; others may specialise in mortgages or insurance.

If you are getting financial advice on retirement saving, you must make sure that the adviser to whom you speak is qualified to give advice on pensions.

There are three types of financial adviser and the type of adviser will affect the range of products that you can be offered.

- **Tied advisers** are able to give advice only on the products that are sold by the company for which they work.

- **Multi-tied advisers** are able to give advice only on the products sold by a limited number of providers.
- **Independent financial advisers (IFAs)** are able to advise you on products from across the whole of the market.

Your adviser must confirm, at the start of your meeting, the range from which he or she is able to select, but if you are at all uncertain, you should ask again.

If a tied or multi-tied adviser cannot offer you a suitable product from the range or company to which he or she is limited, he or she cannot choose the 'next best' thing and must advise you of his or her inability to meet your needs.

Paying for financial advice

There are different ways in which you can pay for financial advice. Normally, your financial adviser will be paid for his or her work by means of either:

- a fee that you agree to pay directly; or
- a commission paid by the provider, should you choose to buy its product on the basis of the adviser's recommendation.

All financial advisers are required to tell you at the start of your first meeting how they will be paid for their work. IFAs are required to offer you a choice between these two options; other types of financial adviser are not able to do so.

Sometimes, you will be offered the option of offsetting a fee against the commission. Because the commission is paid using money from your investment, this means that the cost of the fee will be spread over many years, which can have a negative impact on returns. If you choose instead to pay the fee up-front, the commission will usually be paid back to you.

 Choosing to pay a fee up-front ensures that your adviser will make recommendations without taking into consideration the relative commissions that different products offer.

Most IFAs who charge fees will offer you one free initial session to see whether it is worth taking the consultation further.

Once you get into paid time, you can expect to pay a fee that is upwards of £100 an hour. You will pay more in cities and wealthier parts of the UK.

The fee will be payable whether you buy a product or not.

What do I need to think about?

Before speaking to a financial adviser, it is best to do some preparation, so that you can get the most from your meeting.

You should think about what you are trying to achieve. If you are reading this book, you are almost certainly thinking about saving for retirement. The questions that you may want to ask yourself are therefore as follows.

When am I planning, or hoping, to stop work?

You may aspire to retire as soon as you can afford to do so, or you may want to work as long as you can. But whatever the age at which you are thinking about retiring, you will need to save as much as you can now, while you are working, to give yourself an income when you retire.

Remember: *You cannot normally use a pension scheme to give you an income until you reach the age of 55 (50 until 6 April 2010). Your pension scheme will probably also have rules on when payments start and your State Pension cannot be paid until you reach your State Pension age.*

Make sure that you know from when your pension(s) can be paid and consider how this fits in with your plans.

What level of income can I expect when I retire?

By the time you retire, some costs will have dropped or disappeared completely – for example, if you have a mortgage, you may have paid that off in full.

Some costs may stay the same, such as utility bills.

But other costs could increase – for example, leisure costs, the number of holidays that you take and perhaps the costs of health care.

 Think about the level of income that you will need – and try to be as realistic as possible.

How much have I already saved?

You will need to take stock of the pensions that you have already built up and the value of your other savings. Is the income from these going to be enough?

 Now will be a good time to get up-to-date valuations, including a State Pension forecast.

With what level of risk am I comfortable?

Historically, investments with the most risk have had the potential, over the long term, to produce the best returns.

All types of investment carry a degree of risk (see Chapter 3). 'Safe' investments, for example, may avoid the volatility that is associated with riskier investments that may give higher returns, but the values of even these safe investments run the risk of not keeping up with inflation.

 Think about what level of risk you are comfortable with, taking account of how long you have to save before you retire.

How do I find a financial adviser?

You can search for IFAs in your local area – specifying the areas in which he or she should specialise and the qualifications that he or she should have – online at www.unbiased.co.uk and at www.fsa.gov.uk

Alternatively, you might get a recommendation from a friend who has similar financial needs to yours and who is able to give you the name of an adviser who has served your friend well over a period of time.

When first meeting with a financial adviser

If you are able, you might want to visit an IFA at their office, rather than ask them to come to your home. Some people may feel less sales pressure in an office environment than they do in their own home.

You might want to try out two or three financial advisers, on the basis that the first interview will be free, to see if you like them and understand what they say.

You may want to ask some of the following questions.

- Do you specialise in a particular area, such as pensions for people over the age of 50?
- What experience and qualifications do you have that support that specialist area? (If he or she has neither experience nor qualifications in the relevant area, you should consider going elsewhere.)

The FSA requires that financial advisers have appropriate qualifications when advising in certain specialist areas, such as pensions or **lifetime mortgages** *(see Chapter 9).*

- With how many clients do you personally deal? (If the answer is a very large number, you may want to consider whether the adviser will be able to give you the level of attention and service that you would like.)

- May I speak with a couple of your customers? (A reputable adviser should be happy to put you in touch with other customers, subject to their agreement.)

If you are not satisfied with the answers that you receive or the attitude of the adviser, then you should continue your search. When you are dealing with something as important as your income, you must be confident that your financial adviser is competent and trustworthy.

Buyer beware

Financial advisers have, on occasion, received bad press. You should remember, however, that financial advisers are closely regulated. All should try to do what is best for their customers.

In rare cases, you may need to be aware of the following.

- Be suspicious of any promise of exceptional returns: if a deal sounds too good to be true, it probably is.

- Do not invest in any scheme that you do not understand – particularly if the adviser is vague about the details or does not seem to understand it him or herself.

- Never be rushed into parting with your money because the adviser says that you must take advantage of a special offer immediately.

- Make your cheque out to the firm in which your money will be invested, never to the financial adviser or firm – whatever the reason they may give.

In addition, there is certain advice that you might get that many people, including most financial advisers, would question. Unless you are in particular circumstances that make you different from most members of the public, the following are a few pieces of **bad advice** of which you should beware.

Advice to opt out of a company pension scheme and start a private plan

If you are a member of a company pension scheme, your employer will be paying into it a contribution on your behalf. It is unlikely that your employer will make a similar contribution to a plan that you set up independently – and losing your employer's contribution will be like giving up part of your pay.

If your company pension scheme is a salary-related one (see Chapter 2), your pension benefits are based on your length of service and your pensionable salary. It will be your employer's responsibility to make sure that there is enough money in the pension fund to pay the pension that you build up. It would be very difficult to build up a pension fund on your own that would be sufficient to buy similar benefits when you retire.

In addition, your company pension scheme may have valuable death benefit provisions for your dependants should you die before retirement. These would also be lost if you were to leave the scheme.

Advice to start another personal pension when you already have one

All private individual pension plans (personal, stakeholder and self-invested personal pensions) are subject to the same rules on how and when you can take benefits and how much tax relief your contributions will attract (see Chapter 3). The mechanics of how a fund is built up are also essentially the same.

If you already have a private individual plan, make sure that there are good reasons why your adviser is recommending another plan. There may be valid reasons: for example, some older style personal pensions will increase their charges if you vary or suspend your contribution. It may therefore be appropriate to leave such plans untouched.

But if your adviser recommends that you take out new policies without a valid reason, beware: this could be a rare case of what is called **churning** – that is, a recommendation based only on the fact that the adviser will be getting commission for each policy that he or she sells.

Do you really need a self-invested personal pension (SIPP)?

A self-invested personal pension (SIPP) is a type of personal pension that lets you have more of a say in where your money is invested (see Chapter 3). It is normally only sensible to take out a SIPP if you are comfortable with taking investment decisions, and if you have the time to do the research and to monitor your choices.

If that does not sound like you, and you would rather that someone else were making the investment decisions, then a recommendation to buy a SIPP may seem unsuitable. If your adviser recommends a SIPP to you, but you have no desire to use any of the fancy investment options available, ask your adviser to explain why it is a better choice for you than a stakeholder or personal pension plan.

SIPP policies often pay higher commission. If you are not interested in the greater investment opportunities available through a SIPP, it is possible that there is another reason behind your adviser's recommendation.

Cooling off and cancellation

You normally have a **cooling-off period** during which you can think about the decisions that you have made and cancel any contracts without penalty. Your financial adviser must clearly inform you of the length of cooling-off period that applies (normally, 14 days).

Never be afraid to cancel a contract within that period if you are not completely happy with it –

and never feel obliged to buy anything from an adviser if you are not happy with his or her recommendations.

What can I do if I am unhappy with the advice that I receive?

If you later think that the advice that you have received was unsuitable for you, the firm that advised you will have a complaints procedure in place with which to deal with your complaint. In the first instance, you should set out your complaint in writing to that firm and allow it time in which to respond.

If you are unhappy with its reply, you may be able to ask the Financial Ombudsman Service to investigate (see Chapter 10).

Summary

Getting independent financial advice can be a sensible thing to do if you are at all uncertain about what decisions to take.

Financial advisers are regulated by the Financial Services Authority (FSA), which sets certain standards that they must meet in order to be able to give advice.

Before meeting a financial adviser, it is best to do some preparation, so that you can get the most out of the meeting.

Ten steps to building a retirement saving plan

1. **Don't delay** – The earlier you start planning for your retirement, the easier it will be to build up pension benefits.

2. **Take stock of what you have already built up** – Get up-to-date statements from your pension providers. Find out as much as you can about how your pension scheme works. Get a State Pension forecast.

3. **Think about what lifestyle you want when you retire** – How much income will you need? Remember to take account of your likely State Pension, as well as the savings – including private pensions – that you have built up. What are your costs likely to be? Think about where you spend your money now. Remember that some costs will reduce, but that others could increase.

4. **When do you want to retire?** – Remember, your State Pension is not payable until you reach State Pension age. Private pensions cannot normally pay benefits until you reach the age of 55 (50 until 6 April 2010). Scheme rules may also place restrictions on when a pension is payable.

5. **Is what you have already saved enough?** – Are you already on track? Is the amount that you have already saved going to be enough to give you a comfortable retirement? Be realistic when you think about the answers to these questions.

6. **If not, how much more will you need to save?** – Your pension provider can give you

an illustration of how much pension you could get in the future if you were to save at a certain level.

Quotations will be based on assumptions. There are no guarantees.

7. Build your plan

- Decide when you want to retire.
- Decide how much you will need.
- Work out how much you need to save.
- Work out how much you can afford to save.
- Decide on your saving choices.
- Get advice, if necessary.

8. Carry out your plan

9. Review your plan

- Your circumstances may change.
- Investment conditions may change.
- Your aspirations may change.

It is important that you keep a regular eye on your savings to make sure that you remain on track.

10. Review your plan again – Reviewing your plan is not a one-off exercise: it is important that you review your savings regularly. Make sure that you get regular updates – and seek advice if necessary.

7
The rules

Pensions are notoriously complicated – but they do not have to be. Try thinking of them as simply a savings plan that is designed specifically to give you an income when you retire – one that attracts relatively generous tax relief.

There are, however, rules relating to what you can and cannot do with your pension fund, and this is where it can get complicated. Because the government gives tax relief on pension funds, it imposes rules relating to when and how benefits can be taken, and how much you can save and still enjoy tax advantages.

What can a pension plan pay me?

Pension schemes are designed to pay you an income when you retire. They can also pay some of the benefits as a cash sum (see below).

If you are saving in a salary-related scheme, income must be paid to you by means of a scheme pension – that is, an income that must be paid at least yearly and which cannot be reduced, except in specified circumstances. Such circumstances might, for example, include suspending a pension paid on ill-health grounds because the recipient has now recovered.

If you are saving in a money-purchase scheme, income can be paid by means of a scheme pension, by buying a lifetime annuity or by using an unsecured pension (see Chapter 5).

When can I be paid my pension?

You cannot take benefits from a pension plan before you have reached the age of 55 (50 until 6 April 2010), but you must have started to take them before you reach the age of 75. It is sometimes possible for you to be paid at any age if your health permanently affects your ability to work.

The exact terms on when a pension can be drawn (including on ill-health grounds) will depend on your plan's rules.

How much can I have in cash?

You can usually take up to 25 per cent of the value of your pension fund as a tax-free cash sum and it must normally be paid within 12 months of the date on which you became entitled to your pension.

It may be possible to have your entire fund paid as cash if the total value of all of your private pension plans is worth less than 1 per cent of the lifetime allowance (£1.75 million in 2009–10, meaning that 1 per cent is £17,500).

You must also be over the age of 60 and under the age of 75 if you want to take the whole of your fund as a cash lump sum.

To work out whether you meet the total value test, you need to add up the values of all of your private pensions.

If you are saving in a money-purchase scheme, you will do this simply by using the market values of your fund(s).

If you have benefits from a salary-related scheme, your pension will be valued using a factor of 20:1 – that is, you will need to multiply the pension to which you are entitled by 20. Any pension that was in payment before 6 April 2006 should be valued using a factor of 25:1.

This type of payment is known as a triviality lump sum. You can take 25 per cent of the payment free of tax, but the balance will be taxable as income. If you can choose to take a triviality lump sum, then all similar payments must be made within 12 months of the first.

Luigi has two personal pensions: Plan A is worth £4,000 and Plan B is worth £7,000. In total, Luigi's pensions are therefore valued at £11,000. As long as the plan's rules allow it, Luigi has the option of taking a triviality lump sum from both plans.

If Plan A is paid to Luigi as a triviality lump sum on 22 April 2009, he will need to be paid a triviality lump sum from Plan B paid by 21 April 2010 or he will lose the option.

If a pension scheme is being wound up, it is possible that you might be offered a cash sum in exchange for your pension without having to take account of any other pension plans of which you are a member. This type of payment is known as a winding-up lump sum. Like other trivial payments, you will need to be under the age of 75 to receive it, but you will not need to be over the age of 60.

In addition to the rules above, legislation that took effect at 1 June 2009 means that, from 1 December 2009, occupational pension schemes can offer members a cash sum in exchange for their pension if their pension is worth less than £2,000. If you think that this new legislation may apply to you, you should check with your scheme to see whether it will make such a payment.

Some plans will pay your pension fund entirely as cash if you are suffering from serious ill health. If you want your scheme to consider this option, you will need to give your scheme administrator medical evidence confirming that your life expectancy is less than 12 months.

These are overriding rules by which all pension plans must abide. What your scheme will pay may not be the same as outlined above; instead, any payment will depend on its rules.

How much can I save?

You can save as much as you want towards your retirement. But how much you can save and still get the full tax advantages from which pension funds benefit is limited by two allowances:

- **the lifetime allowance**; and
- **the annual allowance**.

The lifetime allowance

The government limits the total amount of pension saving that you can build up and which can continue to benefit from the permitted tax advantages by means of a lifetime allowance. If the total value of your pension savings is more than this allowance, you could face a tax charge when you take benefits.

The lifetime allowance for 2009–10 was set at £1.75 million and will increase to £1.8 million for 2010–11. It will remain frozen at £1.8 million until at least 2016.

The way in which you will work out the value of your pension, so that you can check how it compares against the lifetime allowance, will depend on the type of scheme of which you are a member.

For money-purchase schemes, the calculation is relatively simple: you simply use the value of your fund at the time that you draw benefits.

If you have pension benefits in a salary-related scheme, they are valued at £20 for each £1 of pension. If you already had a salary-related pension in payment at 5 April 2006, its value will be £25 for every £1 of pension.

On 10 June 2009, **Alison** decides to retire. She is entitled to a pension from her salary-related scheme of £9,250 a year. She also has a stakeholder plan worth £200,000.

Because her stakeholder plan is a money-purchase scheme, the value of her fund is used to test her benefits against the lifetime allowance – that is, £200,000.

The value of her salary-related scheme is calculated using a factor of 20:

£9,250 x 20 = £185,000

In total, Alison's pensions are therefore valued at:

£200,000 + £185,000 = £385,000

For the tax year 2009–10, the lifetime allowance is £1.75 million. Alison has therefore used up only 22 per cent of the lifetime allowance, and so no lifetime allowance charge arises.

What happens if my pension savings are worth more than the lifetime allowance?

A tax charge of 25 per cent is made against the amounts that exceed the lifetime allowance if it is paid as a pension.

If the excess is paid as a lump sum, a further charge of 40 per cent is made, which will make the overall tax charge 55 per cent.

When **Farrukh** retired, the total value of his pension benefits exceeded the lifetime allowance by £10,000. He chose to receive the excess as a lump sum.

The tax charge was calculated as follows:

£10,000 x 25% tax = £2,500 tax

£10,000 – £2,500 = £7,500 lump sum

£7,500 x 40% tax = £3,000 tax

The actual lump sum that Farrukh received was therefore:

£7,500 – £3,000 = £4,500

(The total tax paid was equivalent to a charge of 55 per cent on the excess.)

The annual allowance

There is also a restriction on the annual amount of tax-advantaged pension savings that you can make. This is known as the annual allowance.

For money-purchase schemes, you can check the annual allowance by looking at the total amount of contributions (including any from your employer) that have been paid into a pension plan during the year.

If you are in a salary-related scheme, you will look instead at the increase of your pension and put a value on that increase by using a valuation factor of 10:1.

There is no annual allowance test in the year in which you take your benefits.

For 2009–10, the annual allowance is £245,000. It will rise to £255,000 for 2010–11 and then remain frozen until 2016. If the annual allowance is exceeded, there is a tax charge of 40 per cent on the excess.

Rules on contributions

There is no limit on the amount of contribution that you can make to a pension scheme – but tax relief is limited to gross contributions of up to £3,600 a year, or an amount that is equivalent of 100 per cent of your earnings (subject to UK income tax), whichever is the greater.

To get tax relief on your contributions, you must be a UK resident (or you, or your spouse or civil partner, must be a Crown servant) and be under the age of 75. If you move abroad, you can still claim tax relief, as long as you were a UK resident when you started the plan and as long as you have been a UK resident at some point during the last five years.

Contributions that have not attracted tax relief will not count towards the annual allowance.

Summary

Because the government gives away relatively generous tax relief in relation to pensions, it imposes a number of rules on how and when you can use your pension fund.

These include rules on how much tax relief you can get for your contributions, which is limited by two allowances: an annual allowance and one that is measured over the lifetime of the savings.

There are also limits on how and when benefits can be paid.

8

Know your rights

Introduction

One of the reasons why pensions are notoriously complicated is because, over the years, policymakers have introduced pages and pages of legislation that pension providers must follow.

The purpose of some of that legislation, however, is to give you certain rights.

And as well as the requirements set down in law, the rules of your pension plan may give you rights, depending on your circumstances.

 If you have not yet got a copy, ask your scheme contact for a copy of its explanatory booklet or ask your scheme administrator for a copy of your plan's policy terms. These will explain how your pension should be run.

The purpose of this chapter is to explain some of the more useful rights.

Rights relating to access to a pension scheme

If the company for which you work employs five or more people, your employer should, as a minimum, give you the opportunity to contribute to a stakeholder plan (see Chapter 3). Your employer is not, however, required to contribute to the plan.

In the future, the government intends to make it a requirement that all employees are automatically enrolled into pension schemes. This requirement will include compulsory levels of contributions from both the employee and the employer. It is expected that this will take effect from 2012.

Once the rules on auto-enrolment take effect (see Chapter 2), the requirement for employers to offer their staff access to a stakeholder pension will end.

Rights relating to age discrimination

Since 1 December 2006, it became unlawful for pension schemes to have rules that treat people less favourably, or rules that otherwise disadvantage them, on grounds of age.

The issue of age discrimination and pension schemes is, however, difficult, because so many of the factors involved in the calculation and the payment of pension benefits are linked to age. The legislation therefore includes many exemptions that allow pension schemes to function. And in some cases, discrimination is still permitted if it can be objectively justified.

The practices that are specifically exempted under the regulations, and which are therefore still allowable, include:

- the use of minimum and maximum entry ages into schemes;
- the use of age-related statistics when calculating benefits;
- having a maximum period of service for pension calculations;
- age-related employer contributions, as long as the aim is to give benefits on a more equal basis at retirement; and
- the payment of equal contributions to a money-purchase scheme, even though they will provide different levels of benefit at members' retirements.

Rights in the event of a complaint

If you have a reason to make a complaint, in all cases, it is usually best to try to resolve the matter informally with the party that is the cause of your complaint. But if you are unsatisfied with the outcome of that informal process, you have a right to raise your complaint on a more formal basis.

Company pension schemes must have in place an internal dispute resolution procedure. This can be a one or two-stage process in which your complaint can be formally addressed. Details of to whom you need to write should be included in the initial information that is given to you about the scheme.

If you remain unhappy after completing the internal process, you will normally have the right to ask the Pensions Ombudsman to investigate.

The Pensions Ombudsman will normally expect you to contact the Pensions Advisory Service for help and advice before it will get involved. The Pensions Advisory Service can be contacted at any stage, as long as you have already given the party that is the cause of your complaint the chance to reply.

Both the Pensions Ombudsman and the Pensions Advisory Service share the same address (see Chapter 10).

If you have a complaint about an individual pension plan, you should write to the company that is the cause of your complaint, setting out why you are unhappy. The company should reply to you within eight weeks of receiving your letter and tell you to whom you can now take your complaint if you are still unhappy.

If your complaint concerned the advice that you were given, the Financial Ombudsman Service (see Chapter 10) will be able to investigate.

If your complaint was about the running of your plan – for example, if a mistake was made – it is more likely that the Pensions Ombudsman will be able to deal with it.

Rights in the event of a divorce

If you are divorcing, a court is required to take account of the value of the pensions that you and your ex-partner have built up when sorting out a financial settlement.

It can do this in one of three ways, as follows.

Pension offsetting

Pension offsetting simply means offsetting the value of your pension against your other financial assets, so that any pensions that you hold are left untouched. For example, you might agree to give your ex-spouse the house, in return for keeping all of your pension.

Pension earmarking

From 1 July 1996, it became possible for a court to order that, when pension benefits are eventually paid, part of the benefit is paid to the former spouse. This is known as an **earmarking order**. The pension scheme keeps a copy of the earmarking order, so that it knows what to do when the benefits are payable.

Pension sharing

Pension sharing became possible from 1 December 2000 and allows pension benefits to be shared immediately. This means that some of the value of the member's pension, as decided by the court, is transferred to the ex-spouse.

The ex-spouse can, depending on the rules of the scheme, either use that value to secure new pension rights in the scheme or transfer it into another pension plan.

The member's pension is reduced as a result.

If you are going through a divorce, make sure that your solicitor is taking into account any pension arrangements.

Rights relating to information

As a member of a pension scheme, there is certain information that you must be told on request and other items that you must be told automatically.

The list of things that you are entitled to see is so long that there is no space to list them all in this book.

You will find the full list of information to which you are entitled in the Pensions Advisory Service leaflet, 'Getting information about your occupational pension', available by calling 0845 601 2923 or online at www.pensionsadvisoryservice.org.uk

Rights in the event of maternity leave

If you are a member of a salary-related pension scheme, any period of paid maternity leave that you take should be treated as pensionable service. Your contributions should be based on the pay that you actually receive during your paid maternity leave, but your benefits should continue to be based on your pay before you went on maternity leave.

A period of unpaid maternity leave does not have to be treated as pensionable service.

If you are a member of a money-purchase plan, during a period of paid maternity leave, your rate of contribution will depend on the amount of pay that you are actually receiving. If your employer normally contributes, its contribution should be based on your pay before your maternity leave started. If your employer's contribution was normally dependent upon you also contributing, you will still need to contribute at the agreed percentage (albeit based on a lower rate of pay) for there to be an obligation on your employer to continue paying.

During unpaid maternity leave, neither you nor your employer will be required to contribute.

Some scheme rules are, however, more generous, so you should ask your normal scheme contact about any special terms that apply.

If you are expecting a baby, make sure that you are aware of the rules of your scheme in relation to maternity leave.

Rights relating to part-time employees

It is unlawful to exclude part-time employees from company pension schemes if they are open to full-time employees. There have been a number of court cases dealing with this issue and so, if you have previously been denied membership of a pension scheme simply because you work part-time, you may be able to get backdated membership.

You can find more details about this issue online at www.employmenttribunals. gov.uk

Rights for same-sex partners

Couples who have registered a civil partnership are entitled to the same rights as married couples for survivor's pensions for their civil partners – but this only normally applies to benefits built up after 5 December 2005.

If your pension plan was contracted out (see Chapter 4), your civil partner will be entitled to the same contracted-out benefit rights built up since 6 April 1988 as would be a surviving spouse, as well other pension rights since 5 December 2005.

Some scheme rules are, however, more generous, so you should ask your scheme manager to explain those that apply to your plan.

If you have not registered a civil partnership, your surviving partner may still be entitled to some benefits in the event of your death if the pension scheme normally pays them to unmarried partners.

Schemes can, however, limit the payment of survivor benefits to married spouses and civil partners.

Check what the rules of your scheme say about the rights of your same-sex partner.

Rights in the event of a transfer of employment

If you are a member of a company pension plan and your employment is transferred to a new employer, the new employer is required to provide you with some form of pension (see Chapter 2).

The scheme that the new employer offers must meet certain minimum conditions. If an employer had a contractual obligation to pay into its employee's individual pension plans, the obligation transfers to the new employer.

Summary

The law gives certain rights to people in relation to their pension arrangements, including rights to maternity leave, divorce and equal treatment.

If you want to find out more about your rights in relation to your pension plan, the Pensions Advisory Service offers a comprehensive round-up online at www.pensionsadvisoryservice.org.uk

9

Alternatives to pensions

If you decide that you do not want to put more money into your pension then what else can you do to try to increase your income in retirement?

Other than trusting in luck and the hope that you may benefit from an inheritance, you do have a few options.

Savings

Building up savings outside your pension is an option. If you are still quite a long way from retirement, then you may want to consider saving in stocks and shares (although you should seek independent financial advice before doing this). You should consider moving these into savings as you near retirement.

Individual savings accounts (ISAs) allow you to invest in cash, or in stocks and shares. They are a good way of saving, because any interest and capital gains on your savings are tax-free. The tax on share dividends is also limited, so you may want to consider trying to put the maximum amount into an ISA each year.

Each tax year, you have been allowed to save up to £7,200 in ISAs, of which £3,600 could be in cash. This has, however, now changed.

- From 6 October 2009, if you were born before 6 April 1959, you are able to save up to £10,200 in ISAs, of which £5,100 can be in cash.
- From 6 April 2010, everyone is able to save up to £10,200 in ISAs, of which £5,100 can be in cash.

On retirement, however, you will need to turn your savings into an income. You might simply cash in your savings as you need them – but it is not easy to be certain how much you can draw without running out of money.

The following are some specific income-producing investments that you may want to consider as a way of offering you that certainty:

- British government stocks (known as gilts);
- income bonds; and
- purchased life annuities.

Some savings accounts pay interest monthly and you might consider putting together a package of investments that mature at different times.

If you are interested in putting together a package of different investments, you should seek advice from an independent financial adviser (see Chapter 6).

British government stocks (known as gilts)

British government, or gilt-edged, stocks (known as gilts) are a loan to the British government, repaid for a set price on a set date and paying a fixed income (usually twice a year). You can buy them when they are issued, at a fixed price, or buy them afterwards at a price that may be higher or lower than the issue price. You can buy them through the postal service run for the government by Computershare or through a stockbroker.

The government's Debt Management Office publishes a free guide entitled 'The Private Investor's Guide to Gilts', which is available by calling 0870 703 0143.

Income bonds

Income bonds are available from, amongst other providers, National Savings & Investments (NS&I) and insurance companies.

They work by paying you a regular income, over a fixed term, in return for your investment.

At the end of the term, your investment is repaid.

Purchased life annuities

Annuities (see Chapter 5) can normally only be bought with pension savings, but if you have a lump sum to invest, perhaps from the sale of a house or from an inheritance, you might consider buying a **purchased life annuity.**

Purchased life annuities are sold by insurance companies and, in return for your lump sum, they promise to pay you an income for the rest of your life.

For tax purposes, purchased life annuities are different from pension annuities. The government takes the view that, because your pension savings have already enjoyed tax advantages, income from a pension annuity should be taxed.

As a consequence, while part of the payment from a purchased life annuity is treated as a return of your capital, part is treated as interest. You will be taxed on the interest, but the part that relates to the return of capital will remain tax-free.

Equity release

If you own your own home, this may be a way of generating some money. If you are in receipt of any state benefits, you must consider carefully whether they would be affected if you were to use an equity release scheme.

Although the recent slump in the property market has demonstrated that house prices can fall, depending on its value, you may have the option of releasing some of the **equity** in your home by:

- **downsizing** – that is, selling your home and moving to a smaller property); or
- signing up to an **equity release** scheme, under which the provider pays you cash in return for a share of the equity in your home.

To use an equity release scheme, you usually have to be over a certain age. This will vary, but, typically, you will need to be over the age of 60 to apply for such a scheme.

In addition, some providers will only offer you an equity release scheme if you have no outstanding mortgage held against your property.

There are two main types of equity release scheme:

- **lifetime mortgages**; and
- **home reversion** schemes.

More information and considerations about equity release schemes is available in Age Concern's book Equity Release Made Easy *available by calling 0800 00 99 66 or online at* www.ageconcern.org.uk

Lifetime mortgages

By using a lifetime mortgage, the lender agrees to give you a loan in the form of a lump sum or regular income (or both). You pay no interest on the loan during your lifetime; instead, when you die, the lender will be entitled to take the amount that you have borrowed, plus interest, from the proceeds of the sale of your home.

Home reversion schemes

Under a home reversion scheme, you sell all, or part, of your home to an equity release company, which will pay you a lump sum and/or a regular income in return. In effect, you will no longer own your home – but you will be entitled to remain there as a tenant for the duration of your life without paying rent.

If you are thinking about an equity release scheme, you should seek financial and legal advice first (see Chapter 6) – not least because they can be difficult, expensive or even impossible to get out of should your circumstances change.

More information on what you should take into account is available in Age Concern's two free factsheets, Factsheet 12: 'Raising income or capital from your home' and Factsheet 13: 'Older homeowners – financial help with repairs and adaptations', available by calling 0800 00 99 66 or online at www.ageconcern.org.uk

Summary

Pensions need not be the only way in which you can provide for yourself during your retirement. Other assets that you have can form a significant part of your retirement planning.

Some alternatives are, however, complex and it is worth getting financial advice first.

10
More help

Facts and figures...

The State Pension rates 2009–10	
Basic State Pension	£95.25 a week
Over-80s State Pension	£57.05 a week
Over-80s additional State Pension	£0.25 a week

A **married woman** can claim up to a maximum of £57.05 a week based on her husband's record (her own basic State Pension is topped up to this level, if it is less than this).

From 6 April 2010, a **married man and a civil partner** will similarly be able to claim a basic State Pension that is based on his wife's or his or her partner's record.

Annual increases take effect in April each year. Increases are based on the retail prices index (RPI), subject to a minimum increase of 2.5 per cent.

Pension Credit	
Guarantee Credit	£130.00 a week (single)
	£198.45 a week (couple)
Savings Credit	Up to £20.40 a week (single)
	Up to £27.03 a week (couple)

Private pensions		
	2009–10	2010–11 to 2015–16
The lifetime allowance	£1.75 million	£1.8 million
The annual allowance	£245,000	£255,000
Total value of pension(s) that can be given up for cash	£17,500	£18,000

Useful organisations

Age Concern
For help and advice on issues affecting older people
Freepost (SWB 30375)
Ashburton
Devon TQ13 7ZZ
Tel: 0800 009 966
www.ageconcern.org.uk

Citizens Advice Bureau

For help with money, legal and other problems.
www.citizensadvice.org.uk

Companies House

Crown Way
Cardiff CF14 3UZ
Tel: 0870 333 36 36

Financial Ombudsman Service (FOS)

South Quay Plaza
183 Marsh Wall
London E14 9SR
Tel: 0845 080 1800
Email:
complaint.info@financial-ombudsman.org.uk
www.financial-ombudsman.org.uk
Set up to help to settle disputes between consumers and financial firms, it considers complaints about a range of financial matters – from insurance and mortgages, to savings and investments – and can investigate complaints about the sale or marketing of a pension plan.

Financial Services Compensation Scheme (FSCS)

7th Floor
Lloyds Chambers
Portsoken Street
London E1 8BN
Tel: 020 7892 7300
www.fscs.org.uk
To find out whether or not you are entitled to compensation if your financial provider has gone into liquidation.

Future Pension Centre

The State Pension
Forecasting Team
Tyneview Park
Whitley Road
Newcastle upon Tyne
NE98 1BA
Tel: 0845 3000 168
Textphone: 0845 3000 169
www.direct.gov.uk
To get a forecast of your State Pension.

HM Revenue & Customs

Tel: 0845 302 1479
To check your National Insurance history.

International Pension Centre

Tel: 0191 218 7777
www.direct.gov.uk/ipc/home.asp
For information on State benefits, including the State Pension, for people who live overseas.

Jobcentre Plus

Tel: 0845 055 6688
www.jobcentreplus.gov.uk

For information on working age benefits, such as Child Benefit, Jobseeker's Allowance, etc.

Moneymadeclear
www.moneymadeclear.fsa.gov.uk
For guides and help on a variety of financial issues, including comparing products.

The Pension Protection Fund (PPF)
Knollys House
17 Addiscombe Road
Croydon
Surrey CR0 6SR
Tel: 0845 600 2541
Email: information@ppf.gsi.gov.uk
www.pensionprotectionfund.gov.uk
For information on what help you could get if the company for which you worked went into liquidation and there was not enough money to pay for salary-related pension promises.

The Pension Service
Tel: 0845 606 0265
www.direct.gov.uk
For information about the State Pension, including

finding out about deferring your State Pension.

The Pension Tracing Service
The Pension Service
Tyneview Park
Whitley Road
Newcastle upon Tyne
NE98 1BA
Tel: 0845 600 2537
www.direct.gov.uk
To track down pension plans with which you have lost contact.

The Pensions Advisory Service
11 Belgrave Road
London SW1V 1RB
Tel: 0845 601 2923 (helpline)
Email: enquiries@pensionsadvisoryservice.org.uk
www.pensionsadvisoryservice.org.uk
For information and guidance on all pension schemes, whether State, company or individual, and for help if you have a complaint about your works or private pension plan.

The Pensions Ombudsman
6th Floor
11 Belgrave Road
London SW1V 1RB
Tel: 020 834 9144
Email:
enquiries@pensions-ombudsman.org.uk
www.pensions-ombudsman.org.uk
Completely independent and impartial adjudicator, appointed by the Secretary of State for Work and Pensions to investigate, and decide, complaints and disputes about the way in which pension schemes are run.

The Pensions Regulator
Tel: 0870 606 3636
Email:
customersupport@thepensionsregulator.gov.uk
www.thepensionsregulator.gov.uk
Oversees the running of work-based pension arrangements, but is unable to help individuals in dispute with their pension schemes.

Tax Help for Older People
Pineapple Business Park
Salway Ash
Bridport
Dorset DT6 5DB
Tel: 0845 601 3321
Email:
taxvol@taxvol.org.uk
www.taxvol.org.uk
An independent, free advice service for older people whose household income is less than £17,000 and who cannot afford to pay for professional advice.

Glossary

accrual rate   The proportion of your pensionable earnings that your pension scheme gives you for each year of your membership (eg 1/60th or 1/80th).

added years   The additional pensionable service that you can buy using an additional voluntary contribution (AVC) arrangement.

additional State Pension   A State Pension based on earnings from employment. It is possible to opt out of the additional State Pension.

additional voluntary contribution (AVC)   An arrangement through which you can boost your pension by buying added years (if a salary-related pension scheme) or extra pension income (if a money-purchase pension plan).

alternatively secured pension (ASP)   An alternative to buying an annuity for those aged 75 and over. The rules on alternatively secured pensions are similar to those relating to unsecured pensions, but with different limits.

annual allowance   The maximum amount of yearly tax-advantaged pension savings that you can make.

annuity   An insurance policy that pays an income in retirement.

auto-enrolment   A requirement that all new employees be automatically enrolled in a suitable pension scheme, likely to be in force from 2012.

basic State Pension   The benefit paid at State Pension age to those with a sufficient National Insurance (NI) contribution record.

Bereavement Allowance   A taxable benefit that may be due in the event of the death of a spouse or civil partner, if he or she paid sufficient National Insurance (NI) or if the death was caused by a work-related accident.

Bereavement Payment   A tax-free benefit that may be due in the event of the death of a spouse or civil partner.

bonds   A form of investment that involves loaning funds to the government, a local authority or company, in return for the payment of interest and the return of the original amount at the end of the agreed term.

capital-protected annuity   An annuity that pays a cash lump sum, based on the value used to buy the annuity less the income paid, to your estate in the event of your death before the age of 75.

civil partner   Those in a same-sex relationship who have entered into a civil partnership in accordance with the Civil Partnership Act 2004.

consolidation   The combination of a number of small pension funds into one larger whole, to secure a better deal when using the fund to buy an annuity.

contracting out   The ability to opt out of the additional State Pension and build up benefits in a pension plan instead.

cooling-off period   A statutory period during which you have the right to reconsider the recommendations made to you by a financial adviser and cancel any contract entered into.

death in service   Cover, similar to a life assurance policy, that provides benefits to your dependants or other beneficiaries in the event of your death.

deferring   Choosing to take your State Pension at a later date than that on which you are entitled to take it.

defined-benefit pension scheme   See salary-related pension scheme.

defined-contribution pension scheme   See money-purchase pension plan.

downsizing   The practice of freeing up equity held in a house by buying a smaller house.

earmarking order   An option available to a divorcing couple by which a court order is made that a pension scheme is to pay benefits to a former spouse on the member's retirement.

enhanced annuity   An annuity that pays a higher income if you are overweight or if you smoke.

equities   See shares.

equity   The value that is held in a home less any debt – for example, a mortgage – that may be secured against it.

equity release   A scheme that allows a provider to buy a share of the equity in your home in return for providing you with a lump sum or regular income.

escalating annuity   An annuity that pays out an income that increases over time, either in line with the retail prices index (RPI) or at a fixed rate. Compare with level annuity.

fact find   The information that a financial adviser will seek from you prior to making any recommendation.

final-salary pension scheme   See defined-benefit pension scheme.

Graduated Retirement Benefit (GRB) scheme A form of additional State Pension that was started in 1961, but stopped in 1975.

group personal pension (GPP)   A personal pension that is arranged by an employer for its employees.

Guaranteed Minimum Pension (GMP)   The benefit built up in a salary-related pension scheme before 6 April 1997, as a result of being contracted out of the additional State Pension.

guarantee period   A period during which income from your pension will continue to be paid to your beneficiaries in the event of your death.

Home Responsibilities Protection (HRP)   A scheme introduced in 1978 to protect the contribution records of people with certain caring responsibilities, to be replaced in 2010 with a scheme of National Insurance (NI) credits.

home reversion   A form of equity release in which you sell your home to a provider in return for a lump sum and/or a regular income, and the right to remain in the house until your death.

hybrid pension scheme   A pension scheme that mixes the features of money-purchase pension plans and salary-related pension schemes.

impaired-life annuity An annuity that pays a higher rate of income as a result of a person's serious medical condition.

income bond A form of bond that pays you a regular income, over a fixed term, in return for your investment.

income drawdown See unsecured pension.

income withdrawal See unsecured pension.

independent financial adviser (IFA) A financial adviser who is able to select products from across the marketplace. Compare with multi-tied adviser; tied adviser.

individual savings account (ISA) A form of savings account that benefits from special tax advantages.

investment-linked annuity An annuity from which the income varies according to the performance of the underlying investments.

joint-life annuity An annuity that pays you an income for the duration of your life and, in the event of your death, pays an income to your partner. Compare with single-life annuity.

level annuity An annuity that pays a set amount of income that does not alter over time or with inflation. Compare with escalating annuity.

lifetime allowance The maximum amount of lifetime tax-advantaged pension savings that you can make.

lifetime mortgage A form of equity release in which the lender gives you a loan in return for the right to take that amount plus interest, from the proceeds of the sale of your home on your death.

market value reduction (MVR)   A reduction in the value of a with-profits fund that may be used to reflect underlying market conditions if the plan is used to pay benefits at a time other than your selected retirement age.

money-purchase pension plan   Also known as defined-contribution pension scheme, this is a pension scheme in which a fund builds up, based upon the contributions saved. On retirement, the fund is used to give an income either by buying an annuity or by means of an unsecured pension. Compare with salary-related pension scheme.

multi-tied adviser   A financial adviser who is able to select products from the ranges offered by only a small number of providers. Compare with independent financial adviser (IFA); tied adviser.

National Insurance (NI)   Payments that are deducted from your pay or declared through self-assessment. Rights to certain State Pension benefits, including the State Pension itself, are based on your NI contribution history.

National Insurance (NI) credit   A system under which, depending on your circumstances, you are credited as paying National Insurance (NI).

occupational pension scheme   A scheme that is set up by an employer for the benefit of its employees. (Also refers to schemes set up by the government for workers in the public sector.)

open market option (OMO)　Your right to shop around for an annuity rather than to buy your annuity only from your pension provider.

pension offsetting　An option available to a divorcing couple by which the value a person's pension rights are offset against other assets as part of a divorce settlement.

pension sharing　An option available to a divorcing couple by which part of the value of a person's pension is transferred to his or her former spouse and new pension rights created.

pensionable salary　The earnings used to work out retirement benefits in a salary-related pension scheme.

pensionable service　The length of time used to work out retirement benefits in a salary-related pension scheme.

Pension Credit　A means-tested benefit that makes sure that people over the age of 60 have a minimum level of income. It comprises two elements: the Guarantee Credit and the Savings Credit.

personal pension　A type of money-purchase pension plan taken out by individuals.

protected rights　The fund built up in a money-purchase pension plan from rebates paid as a result of contracting out of the additional State Pension.

purchased life annuity　An annuity bought from an insurance company using private savings (rather than pension savings), in return for which it will pay you an income for the rest of your life.

qualifying year   A tax year during which your earnings are more than the lower earnings limit that is set by the government.

retail prices index (RPI)   The average measure of change in the prices of goods and services bought in the UK.

salary-related pension scheme   Also known as a final salary or defined-benefit pension plan, this is a pension scheme that calculates benefits based upon your length of service and salary. Compare with money-purchase pension plan.

self-invested personal pension (SIPP)   A type of personal pension that lets the policyholder have more control over in what he or she invests.

shares   A form of investment that involves the ownership of a small part of a public company, the value of which can go up or down.

short-term annuity   An annuity that pays income for a fixed duration, eg five years.

single-life annuity   An annuity that pays you an income for the duration of your life, but stops in the event of your death. Compare with joint-life annuity.

stakeholder pension   A low-cost type of personal pension that has limits on the level of charges that can be made.

State Earnings-Related Pension Scheme (SERPS)   The name given to the additional State Pension between 6 April 1978 and 5 April 2002.

State Second Pension (S2P)   The name given to the additional State Pension since 6 April 2002.

State Pension age   The age at which you are entitled to your State Pension (presently 65 for men and 60 for women, but due to change from 2010).

tied adviser   A financial adviser who is able to select products from the range offered by only one provider. Compare with independent financial adviser (IFA); multi-tied adviser.

transfer value   This is the value of the pension rights that you have built up that is available for transfer to another pension scheme.

triviality lump sum   A lump sum that can be paid in exchange for your pension if the total value of all of your pension funds is no more than a certain amount and if certain other conditions are met.

unsecured pension   An alternative way in which to receive an income without buying an annuity, for those between the ages of 55 (50 until 6 April 2010) and 75.

voluntary contribution   A payment that you may choose to make to plug any gaps in your National Insurance (NI) record and improve your basic State Pension.

Widowed Parent's Allowance   A taxable benefit that may be payable to those under State Pension age and in receipt of Child Benefit in the event of the death of a spouse or civil partner.

working life   The period of your life during which you are considered able to work (presently 49 years for a man and 44 years for a woman).

Index

A

Abroad, retiring 13
Accrual rate,
    salary-related pensions 26,
    131
Added years, work pensions
    35–36, 131
Additional State Pension
    see State Second Pension
    (S2P)
Additional voluntary
    contribution (AVC)
    schemes 35–38, 131
Age
    annuities 73
    contracting out 69
    discrimination 112–113
    for obtaining individual
      pensions 57–58
    for obtaining State
      Pension 2
    for obtaining work
      pensions 27–28, 33
    to receive benefits from
      a pension 104
    to receive lump sums 104
Alternatively secured pensions
    (ASPs) 82, 83–84, 131
Annual allowance, tax relief
    51, 109, 131
Annual statements,
    individual pensions 63
Annuities 32–33, 57, 72–73,
    131
    alternatives to 81–84
    death after buying 78
    different types of 74–78
    ill health 73, 79

    purchased life 122–123
    shopping around 79–80
    when to buy 73
Attendance Allowance 4, 5
Auto-enrolment, 2012,
    work pensions 44–45, 131

B

Basic State Pension *see*
    State Pension, basic
Benefits
    Attendance Allowance
      4, 5
    Carer's Allowance 11
    Child Benefit 4, 5, 11
    Constant Attendance
      Allowance 4, 5–6
    Disability Living Allowance
      4, 6
    Income Support 4
Bereavement Allowance
    18, 132
Bereavement Payment 19,
    132
Bonds, investing in 54, 132
British government stocks
    122

C

Capital-protected annuities
    76–77, 132
Carer's Allowance 11
Cash, investing in 53–54
Cash sums *see* lump sums
Child Benefit 4, 5, 11
Churning 98
Civil partnerships 132

The four national Age Concerns in the UK have joined together with Help the Aged to form new national charities dedicated to improving the lives of older people.

Age Concern Books

Age Concern Books publishes a wide range of titles that help thousands of people each year. They provide practical, trusted advice on subjects ranging from pensions and planning for retirement, to using a computer and surfing the internet. Whether you are caring for someone with a health problem or want to know more about your rights to healthcare, we have something for everyone.

Ordering is easy To order any of our books or request our free catalogue simply choose one of the following options:

☎ Call us on **0870 44 22 120**

🖱 Visit our website at **www.ageconcern.org.uk/bookshop**

✉ Email us at **sales@ageconcernbooks.co.uk**

You can also buy our books from all good bookshops.